Kundalini's Grace Revealed
in the Light of Advaita

*'Ya Devi Sarvabhuteshu Shakti-rupena Samsthita
Namastasyai Namastasyai Namastasyai Namo Namah.'*

'To the Divine Mother who dwells within all beings
as sacred power, energy and inner strength,
we offer endless reverence and humble salutations.'

—*Durga Saptashati*

Kundalini's Grace Revealed
in the Light of Advaita

Dr Kunwar Singh

YogiImpressions®

YogiImpressions®

KUNDALINI'S GRACE REVEALED IN THE LIGHT OF ADVAITA

First published in India in 2026 by
Yogi Impressions LLP
1711, Centre 1, World Trade Centre,
Cuffe Parade, Mumbai 400 005, India.
Website: www.yogiimpressions.com

First Edition, January 2026

ISBN 978-93-94515-94-9

Printed at: TACT Print

MEDICAL DISCLAIMER

This book reflects a lived experience of the *Kundalini* process and is meant to simply offer support and perspective to those walking this path. By no means is it offering any medical or professional advice.

If you are facing physical or psychological challenges, please consult a qualified doctor or healthcare professional. Do not stop or delay medical treatment, thinking the contents of this book will serve the purpose. Doctors and medical professionals remain essential for safeguarding health and well-being.

DEDICATION TO THE GURU

I bow in deepest gratitude to you, my *guru*, Gautam Sachdeva. Without your guiding presence, this book would never have been possible, nor would my life have unfolded in sanity throughout the turbulence of the Kundalini process.

When the energy rose like a storm, tearing apart my mind and body, you didn't offer me techniques or promises but something much more valuable—the simplicity of *Advaita*. Through your compassion, I learned not to cling to bliss, nor fear the fire and overwhelming experiences that the Kundalini process brought with it. Your clarity anchored me when I was drowning in visions and despair.

You taught me that I am not the doer, that life lives itself, and that what I truly AM is untouched by the storm. That teaching was not merely abstract; it was very much practical as it saved me from being consumed by the very process meant to liberate me.

You were the steady flame when I was lost in darkness and the mirror that reflected the Truth when I was blind to It. Whatever words I write here, they rest on the foundation of your grace.

This book is therefore offered to you as a token of my immeasurable appreciation and gratefulness.

Contents

Foreword

When Kundalini awakens in a sincere seeker, it acts as an inner guide, quietly illuminating the path beyond the mind and into subtler realms of existence. With this awakening, there often comes a flood of questions calling for clarity, integration and guidance. This is when the presence of a true guru becomes essential, whether in physical form or through the quiet grace that arrives when the disciple is ready. Dr Kunwar Singh's journey is a reflection of this sacred process.

From a young age, Dr Singh was stirred by soul-level questions about life, death and the purpose of existence—questions that later paved the way for a spontaneous Kundalini awakening. Though untrained in any formal spiritual practice, his inner transformation began to unfold naturally, perhaps as a result of *karmic* readiness or past-life maturity. At a pivotal moment, the teachings of Advaita entered his life through his guru, catalysing an inner recognition of truths he had long sought. What emerged from the whole process is this book, a personal yet universally resonant account of spiritual awakening, written not to instruct but to offer a clear window into the often unseen terrain of inner transformation. It is free from dogma, grounded in direct experience and refreshingly sincere.

What makes Dr Singh's path remarkable is the natural integration of the three paths of Jnana (Knowledge), Bhakti (devotion) and *Karma* (action)—a harmony long emphasized by sages like *Ramana Maharshi*. His awareness, devotion to the guru and application of Advaita in daily life reflect a rare alignment of grace, readiness and sincerity. Having supported many on the path of Kundalini awakening, I recognize the rarity of such a journey.

This book is a testament to that divine alignment, offering genuine seekers both guidance and inspiration. The spiritual path is not linear. It is, as the scriptures say, like walking a razor's edge. Yet, with surrender, faith and love, it becomes a journey of profound reward. Dr Singh is one of the few who have asked life's deepest questions and been graced with glimpses of the answers.

May this work serve as both a mirror and a guide, and may your own seeking continue—with trust, humility and open-hearted surrender.

Santosh Sachdeva
Author of *The Kundalini Trilogy*

Acknowledgements

This book could not have come into being without the grace and support of many who have walked alongside me on this journey.

First and foremost, I bow in deepest gratitude to Gautam Sachdeva, whose guidance has been a lamp in the midst of my turbulent Kundalini journey. Through his peaceful and grounding presence, untouched by phenomena, and his simple yet profound Advaitic teachings, he has shown me the way to peace, clarity and stillness.

I wish to acknowledge my parents, who have stood by me with love and support. Though initially hesitant about my writing and sharing this book with others, they eventually embraced the journey with me and encouraged me wholeheartedly.

I offer my heartfelt thanks to Santosh Sachdeva, Gautam*ji*'s mother, whose pioneering works on the subject of Kundalini were among my earliest inspirations. It was through her YouTube channel that I was first led to Gautamji's teachings, and for this divine thread of connection, I remain ever grateful.

To Devika Khanna, Gautamji's wife, I extend my warm appreciation for the compassion with which she shares him with all of us (students and disciples), allowing us to receive the blessings of his presence.

I am also grateful to members of our community, including Meenakshi Rawa, Aritra Choudhury and Fida Shaw, as well as many others who have been pillars of friendship and support along the way.

I especially wish to express my gratitude to my editor, Mehernosh Unwalla, who taught me how to organize my spiritual catharsis—my raw outpourings—into a coherent, readable form. With immense patience and kindness, he guided me to work slowly, carefully and methodically. Despite my imperfect grammar and tendency to forget things, he remained steady, supportive and encouraging.

Both Gautam and Mehernosh, in their own ways, gave me an unexpected course in writing, publishing, formatting and viewing a book from the reader's perspective. Mehernosh is not only an editor but also a friend who has taught me invaluable lessons about life in addition to the craft of bookmaking.

Above all, I bow to the entire *Guru Parampara*, the unbroken lineage of wisdom and love, whose blessings have carried me through shadow and light.

I thank not only those who supported me, but also those who tested me, challenged me and were even unkind to me. They, too, were teachers—blessings in disguise—who helped me grow in forgiveness, compassion and transcendence.

Finally, I offer gratitude to all the beautiful souls, known and unknown, who have touched my life in ways small and great. This book is as much theirs as it is mine.

What Is Kundalini?

The word 'Kundalini' is derived from the Sanskrit word '*kundal*', meaning 'coiled up'. The primordial cosmic energy, also known as the Serpent Power, is the fundamental life force and, at the same time, the supreme spiritual energy usually lying dormant and coiled three-and-a-half times at the base of the subtle spine.

Kundalini is not just energy but the living presence of the sacred within every human being. In its sleeping state, it holds the potential for spiritual awakening, waiting for the individual's preparedness, characterized by the right balance of devotion, purity and awareness. When it begins to rise, it leads the seeker from the sense of 'I', of being an individual entity, towards the vast Knowledge that all is One. This awakening cannot be forced through sheer effort; it unfolds naturally through surrender, love and inner readiness.

As Kundalini rises through the *Sushumna Nadi* (the central channel of the subtle spine), it passes through the *chakras* (energy centres), one by one. Each chakra opens a new realm of perception. The lower centres deal with survival, desire and will, while the higher ones awaken compassion, clarity and divine wisdom. This process purifies both body and mind, balancing the subtle flow of the life force. It is both scientific and sacred. On the physical level, it refines the nervous system.

On the spiritual level, it dissolves the illusion of separation between the self and the Divine.

True Kundalini awakening happens through grace and guidance, and not by force or reckless experimentation. The energy rises gently and safely when awakened through devotion, meditation, the blessings of a realized guru, or a spiritual practice that has its roots in the guru's parampara and is, therefore, time-tested. The guru's presence acts as a steady light, keeping the seeker balanced, as old patterns dissolve and deeper energies awaken. This kind of awakening nurtures peace, clarity and inner strength.

By contrast, trying to awaken Kundalini forcefully—for example, through drugs, intense breath control or ungrounded techniques—can be dangerous. These methods can overstimulate the body and mind, leading to confusion, anxiety or even lasting mental and physical disturbances. It is also possible that Kundalini can rise accidentally, as it happened in my case during the practice of *trataka* (candle gazing), which one would take to be a harmless *yogic* practice. The energy of Kundalini is powerful and sacred; without purity, preparation and guidance, it can become overwhelming rather than enlightening.

In the light of the wisdom of Advaita, Kundalini and *Consciousness* are one: The movement of *Shakti* (divine energy) and the stillness of *Shiva* (Awareness) are not two separate entities but two aspects of the same Truth. When the energy reaches the crown of the head, all opposites dissolve. In this state of *Nirvikalpa Samadhi,* there is no longer seeker or sought but only the quiet radiance of the One.

Many *Hatha Yoga* and *Kundalini Yoga* traditions think of the crown as the final destination. However, a stable state of *Sahaja Nirvikalpa Samadhi* (ongoing effortless *samadhi*) results with the permanent death of the ego, when Kundalini descends through the *Amrita Nadi* into the cave of the Heart (not the physical heart but the Spiritual Heart or Consciousness Itself), which is different from the *Heart Chakra*. In this state, one continuously abides as Consciousness while operating in everyday life. This process happens by grace alone and has been testified not only by Ramana Maharshi but also by Saint Kabir and Guru Nanak Devji.

Santosh Sachdeva, the author of *The Kundalini Trilogy* and an authority on the subject,* has this to say about operating from the Spiritual Heart after experiencing the highest state of Consciousness:

> When a *yogi* reaches the *Sahasrara Chakra* (the Crown Chakra), they experience profound stillness and bliss in full awareness: the thoughtless state, where the mind is completely still. This is a state of nothingness—a state of soundless silence. No day or night, no dusk or dawn. It just *is*.
>
> To permanently remain in this state would require complete dissolution, which, in turn, requires further ascension. So, for example, I, as a householder yogi, would opt to descend back into the Spiritual Heart from the Crown Chakra, where there is oneness and a feeling of love, and I would operate from there. As Sant Dnyaneshwar says, alone there is no happiness, so God created another.

The journey of Kundalini is not a single event but a continuous deepening. With each act of surrender, the divine presence grows stronger. The seeker comes to realize that the same power rising within us also gloriously pervades all of

* Refer to the foreword of this book.

Creation. Life itself becomes worship. In this awakening, there is no struggle, no fear—only the living grace of Consciousness unfolding as peace, love and unity.

Who Should Read This Book

This book is not written for casual readers or those seeking entertainment through spirituality. It is meant for

- ❖ those whose lives have been touched by the raw intensity of Kundalini awakening and feel shaken, bewildered or broken by the mystery;
- ❖ seekers of Truth, who long for what lies beyond the mind and its restless search;
- ❖ those who, having undergone Kundalini awakening, face visions, bliss, fear and despair;
- ❖ students of Advaita, who wish to see how non-duality can illuminate even the fiercest storms of awakening;
- ❖ devotees of the *Divine Mother*, who want to bow more deeply to Her, not only in bliss but even when the fire of Kundalini is raging;
- ❖ those in suffering, who search for meaning in their pain, and who may discover that even anguish can be grace.

This book is not meant to glorify my journey but to remind you of your own. Whatever shape your awakening takes, know this: You are not alone. Others have walked through the fire and found peace on the other side. The path may strip you bare, but it never abandons you. The Mother's work is merciful, even when it feels unbearable.

May this guidebook offer comfort, clarity and companionship on the path. Above all, may it point you, as Gautam Sachdeva pointed me, to the silent presence that cannot be lost.

Introduction

This book was not planned. It was born of necessity.

Since childhood, I was always full of questions. My family often grew irritated at my constant enquiries, especially my favourite one: 'Where have I come from?' My mother would answer, 'From my belly.' To which I would innocently reply, 'Then I want to return to it.'

Unlike many spiritual authors who describe extraordinary visions or mystical childhood experiences, my early years were simple. Yet, there was always an undercurrent of unease, a curiosity that wouldn't let me rest. I carried a deep fear of death, and every few months, I would slip into a blank, thoughtless state. Instead of bringing me peace, these episodes left me terrified, throwing me into waves of panic until they subsided.

I often wondered about the point of all this living. I would tell my friends, 'After seventy years, none of us will even be here. So why all this competition, hatred and self-importance?' These questions made me contemplative, reserved and inwardly turned, but they also left me feeling alienated from the rest of the world.

Being overly sensitive, withdrawn and of a delicate nature, I was incessantly bullied by my peers and teachers in school. Though painful, this became a hidden blessing: the harshness outside turned me inward. While others sought worldly possessions, I immersed myself in poetry, philosophy, Indian mythology and reflections on *karma* and past lives. I had no fascination for temples or *gurdwaras*, nor did I pursue rituals. My only compass was the quiet conviction that I should not do wrong, even if others wronged me.

I longed for validation and tried hard to fit in, but in the end, I often walked away disappointed. Friends were few, but the two who stayed with me became lifelines. Looking back, I know their companionship saved me from slipping into depression and suicidal despair. Even today, their families lovingly ask why I give so much of myself to them, and I smile silently in response. For me, it is simply a karmic exchange, since their friendship once saved my life. My love for them is a reciprocation.

During my pre-college years, I drew solace from books, such as *Chicken Soup for the Soul*. In my first year of college, I turned to the Bhagavad Gita, reading it every day with deep devotion. Around this time, in 2017, I began practising trataka to improve my concentration as well as my eyesight. I did not know then that this simple exercise would ignite the fire of Kundalini within me, setting me on a journey of bliss, terror and grace.

Bliss, visions or extraordinary powers. This is what seekers often imagine Kundalini to be. But the reality is quite different. It can be a walk through hell on the way to heaven.

Kundalini is fire—unpredictable, overwhelming and often merciless. She strips away illusions, burns through conditioning and leaves you naked before the Truth.

For me, this process was both terrifying and transformative. Sometimes, I felt I would go insane, be consumed by an energy I could not control, or even die. At other times, waves of bliss intoxicated me so completely that I longed for nothing else. The pendulum of fire and nectar left me bewildered.

Though my heart leaned naturally towards *Vedanta*, after the Kundalini awakening, I experimented endlessly—through books, techniques and practices—without guidance from anyone else. The ride was bumpy and full of trial and error. Till I met my guru.

The saving grace was meeting Gautam Sachdeva in person, in 2021. His simple guidance, rooted in the tradition of Advaita, lived by him as well as his predecessors—Siddharameshwar Maharaj, Nisargadatta Maharaj and Ramesh Balsekar—became my anchor. 'Whatever comes and goes is not real. You are not the doer.' These words, which guide many seekers who come to Gautam, were not ideas; they were a lifeline. They helped me walk through visions, despair and the temptation of acquiring powers, without losing my balance.

Gautamji's steady guidance became the balancing force that kept me from being consumed by the fire and helped me return again and again to stillness. Nevertheless, the four years before meeting him were very chaotic and turbulent. This just goes to show the immense importance of a living guru.

The Kundalini journey left me raw, broken, confused and often desperate. Nights without sleep, days of unbearable energy surges and visions that terrified me—all of this pressed me to seek clarity. What emerged from this chaos as well as

Gautamji's guidance was writing: an attempt to articulate the inexpressible.

The account of my journey that follows is neither theory nor philosophy. It is a lived truth, shaped by fire and soothed by silence. It is the path of Kundalini, envisioned and stabilized through the light of Advaita. If I had relied only on the mind, I would have drowned in experiences. But by the grace of Gautam Sachdeva, I discovered the stillness in which even fire cannot burn.

The pages herein weave together despair and ecstasy, visions and silence, the ego and surrender. They bear testimony to the guru's steady pointing and the fierce compassion of the Divine Mother, or *Ma Kali* (Kundalini). She is deeply loving and fiercer than you can imagine. She ruthlessly dispels illusion.

Part I of this book is about my Kundalini experience. Part II and III comprise poems dedicated to the Divine Mother and the guru respectively, which I felt compelled to write after the experience. Part IV is an attempt to guide those who are on the Kundalini journey and need answers to some questions that give them sleepless nights (apart from the journey itself doing so).

The text contains a substantial number of non-English words and spiritual terminology in particular. Hence the reader (especially those who are unfamiliar with this terrain) will find it helpful to refer to the glossary at the end. All the first instances of the words therein appear in italics in the text (and vice versa in passages where the rest of the text is italicized).

This book is both a memoir and an offering. It speaks of my Kundalini journey in the light of my guru's Advaitic wisdom, where nothing needs to be attained but all that is false is surrendered at the altar of Truth. It is offered to the reader as a hand stretched out in the dark to comfort them; to make them feel that there's a compassionate voice telling them, *You are not alone. Know that the fire will eventually embrace you as grace.*

My words serve as both witness and companion to anyone walking this fierce yet merciful and divine path. If they bring comfort to even one seeker who feels lost on the path of Kundalini, then this book's purpose is fulfilled.

Dr Kunwar Singh

Shiva becomes capable of Creation only when united with Shakti; otherwise, even the Lord is not able to stir. Therefore, how can one who does not do good deeds or sing Your praises become adequate to worship You, O Goddess of mine, who is worshipped by the Trinity.

—Adi Shankaracharya
***Saundarya Lahiri*, Verse 1**

PART I

MY KUNDALINI EXPERIENCE

1

The First Stirring of the Journey

As far as I can remember, there was a restlessness in me that nothing could ease. While others were absorbed in studies, friendships or small joys, I carried a silent ache, a question that refused to leave me: *What is the purpose of all this? Why am I here? What lies beyond death?*

These were not mere thoughts. They were like a flame in the heart, a longing that made it impossible to rest on the surface of life. Though I did not understand it then, this yearning was the first stirring of Kundalini, the subtle whisper of the Divine Mother, drawing me inward towards the Truth.

At that time, I did not know how to find the silence I was being called into. But something was already moving within, waiting for the moment when the hidden current would burst open.

First Lightning

When Kundalini finally decided to rise within me, it was without warning. I was practising trataka to improve my eyesight and concentration. I never knew it was a Hatha Yoga practice that could lead to an accidental Kundalini awakening. A surge of golden energy shot through me like lightning, splitting open the world I had known. My breath caught, thoughts stopped and, for a few timeless moments, there was only light.

In that flash, the little self (the individual) I had believed myself to be, seemed to burn away. There was overwhelming bliss and, at the same time, terror. I felt I was dissolving into nothingness. Yet, even in that annihilation, there was completeness. If death had come in that instant, it would not have mattered, for all was already whole.

Then, just as suddenly, the experience passed. The mind returned with its questions: *What was that? Where has it gone? How can I get it back?* That was the beginning of the long and unpredictable journey of Kundalini awakening.

Seed of Surrender

In those early days, I thought I had 'achieved' something. I longed for a repeat performance—to capture the experience once again. I did not yet understand that no effort of mine could summon it, because it had never been 'mine' to begin with.

Years later, sitting with Gautamji, I heard words that pierced my very core: 'All functioning belongs to the Divine and not to the individual. The sense of being a separate doer is the root illusion. Life is lived through us, not by us.'

Those words struck me because they described exactly what my first awakening had shown me. The lightning had come unbidden. I had not called it, nor could I command it. Something vast had moved, and I was powerless before it. This was the first hint that the journey ahead would not be about control; what was required was surrender. But back then, I did not realize it.

In Retrospect

Now, when I look back at those first stirrings, I see clearly that both sides of the path were already present. Kundalini revealed itself as fire, burning away all that was false. But hidden in that fire was the Truth of Advaita: What I sought was ever present.

The golden lightning was not the beginning of something new but the unveiling of what had always been here. It was the crack in the shell of the 'I', through which I could glimpse that life is not what the mind imagines.

The journey had begun, not towards achievement but towards the dissolving of all illusion, until only the Truth constantly remains.

2

The Unpredictable Energy of Kundalini

At first, Kundalini's awakening was like being embraced by heaven itself. Waves of bliss coursed through my body, dissolving every boundary of who I thought I was. The mind, once a restless chatterbox, fell into silence without effort. In its place arose a luminous presence—alive, gentle and vast.

Colours around me seemed to shine with a deeper beauty. The sound of a bird, the rustle of leaves, the laughter of a child; they all carried a sweetness I had never noticed before. My body felt light, as if I were walking on air. At times, I wondered if paradise had descended into me.

For a while, I lived intoxicated by this sweetness. I thought the journey would continue like this: a steady unfolding of light and bliss.

But I was soon to learn that Kundalini is never predictable. It does not move according to the mind's wishes. It comes to purify, to dismantle, to tear down every falsehood. Bliss is only one of its aspects, and to experience it, illusions and fears need to be transcended.

Bliss Becomes Fire

The shift was shocking. The same energy that had poured nectar throughout my body suddenly burst into flames. What had felt like benediction now felt like unbearable heat.

Nights became my greatest trial. I would lie awake for hours, feeling currents of electricity rushing through every nerve. Sleep became impossible. My body jerked, as if invisible hands were shaking me. Strange inner sounds filled my ears—ringing bells, distant birds and even chanting that had no source in the outer world.

Sometimes, as I sat still, I felt fingers combing gently through my hair, though no one was there. At other times, a sharp burning rose up my spine, so intense that I thought my body might burst into fire.

The mind, frightened and confused, began to ask, *Have I done something wrong? Am I being punished? Am I going mad?*

This was the first time I tasted the other side of Kundalini. Fire. And this fire was merciless in challenging the ego, ignorance and illusions.

Flurry of Visions

Along with this turbulence came visions. Night after night, my dreams carried powerful symbols, as though the unconscious itself was being cleansed. These are some of the dreams I had:

Snakes slithering out of a suitcase, coiling and uncoiling like the energy inside me. Being in a taxi full of snakes. Although these snakes were biting me, I did not experience any fear. Being in a situation where fire was raging behind me, chasing me through landscapes, from which I could not escape. Riding a white horse into a church, only to watch the roof explode open, as though every structure of belief was being torn apart. Collapsing or exploding buildings as well as crashing airplanes.

These dreams symbolize the crumbling and disintegration of the dense ego structure.

Sometimes, my past lives appeared before me: scenes of suffering, unfinished karma and echoes of forgotten identities, which were all demanding to be burned and released. These visions were so vivid that their after-effects lingered during my waking hours.

At first, I clung to these visions, believing they carried messages of deep significance. I wrote them down, tried to interpret them and even looked upon them as signs of spiritual progress. But, over time, I began to see what Gautamji would later confirm. These were simply the mind's way of processing the fire of transformation. They were not the Truth per se but only Its manifestation.

Long Nights of Fear

Nights were often unbearable. At times, lying in darkness, I felt sure my mind would crumble to pieces. Tremors shook my body, my heart raced uncontrollably and my breath grew shallow. There were moments when I thought, *I will not survive this. I will combust. I will die.*

And yet, death did not come. Morning always broke, and with it, a strange gratitude: *Yet another day to walk through this fire.*

Mixed Blessing

Looking back, I can see that the Divine Mother was teaching me through both sweetness and terror. She intoxicated me to win my trust, burnt me to cleanse me, tempted me with powers to expose my pride and then humbled me into surrender.

What seemed like chaos was, in truth, perfect choreography. Every high, every low, every vision, every nightmare was Her way of dismantling illusions.

I began to notice a subtle shift. The questions that plagued me—*How can I control this? How can I stop the fire? How can I bring back the bliss?*—gradually transformed into a different attitude: *Let it come. Let it burn. Let it pass.* This was not resignation but surrender. A quiet recognition that the energy was wiser than me, that it knew exactly what to burn and what to reveal.

'Do not measure your progress by experiences. What comes will go. What is constant cannot be lost.' These words by Gautamji became my lifeline. They turned my gaze away from visions and towards the silent ground in which all visions dissolve.

Today, when I look back at those early storms, I see them not as punishment but as mercy. Without the burning, my pride would not have been exposed. Without the insomnia, I would not have learnt to rest in awareness instead of sleep. Without the visions, I would not have seen how easily the ego can disguise itself in spiritual clothing.

The Divine Mother was teaching me in Her fierce language. Every tear, every tremor, every sleepless night was Her way of preparing the ground for something deeper.

The unpredictable energy of Kundalini was not against me. It was *for* me. It was the fire that stripped me of everything false, so that the Eternal Truth could shine by Itself.

3

The Ego's Return on Attaining Powers

As the current of Kundalini continued to surge through me, I was drawn deeper into territories I had never imagined. The fire that had set my body and dreams aflame, now began to open hidden dimensions of perception. It was as if veils were being lifted, one by one, revealing layers of existence not normally accessible to the five senses.

Special Abilities Surface

I began to see auras, which were subtle initially. I could see a faint shimmer around people, like light caught at the edge of vision. Then, slowly, it grew clearer, becoming auras of colour. These auras would correspond to the moods of people: They glowed when joy was present and dimmed when sorrow arose. Blue radiance wrapped around a calm friend. Golden hues shimmered around someone in devotion. Dense, murky shades clung to those in pain.

I was astonished. It felt as though the secret life of the world had been revealed to me. What people tried to hide in their words could not be hidden in the colours that surrounded them. It was like seeing with new eyes: a window into the truth behind appearances.

Alongside this came an awakening of intuition. I would know what someone was about to say before they spoke. I would sense the heaviness or lightness in a room the moment I entered. Sometimes, my hands moved instinctively towards the body of someone in distress, as if guided to the places where energy was blocked. A warmth or tingling would spread through my palms, and the other person would sigh in relief, unaware of the invisible healing taking place.

Drawn by this sensitivity, I began to explore *Tarot*. The cards became more than symbols—they were living mirrors. When I laid them out, meanings would flow without effort, not from a study of the subject but from an inner knowing that seemed to speak through me. Each reading revealed uncanny insights, leaving me humbled and bewildered.

Subtle Poison of Specialness

To anyone else, these abilities might have seemed like gifts. But to me, they felt like a door opening into mystery. I believed I had entered a higher stage on the spiritual path and that these 'powers' were proof of progress. A dangerous seed had taken root. The ego, which I thought had been humbled by Kundalini's fire, returned in a subtler form.

I began to feel different from others. Outwardly, I still appeared humble and bowed to the Divine Mother in devotion. But inwardly, there was a quiet pride: *I can see what others cannot. I can sense energies. I can heal. I am chosen for something special.*

It was intoxicating. I looked forward to visions, readings and moments of insight. I meditated not only to surrender but to sharpen these powers. (But, of course, at that time, I was blissfully oblivious to the glaring contradiction in doing so.) The mind that once clung to bliss now clung to powers. It had found a new toy to hold on to.

What I did not see then was that this pride was as binding as any worldly attachment. The chains were made of light, but they were still chains.

Guru's Words Ring True

At this critical crossroads, the grace of my guru entered my life more deeply. Gautamji, with his calm and gentle presence, listened to me as I enthusiastically revealed my special abilities to him. But instead of encouraging them, he placed before me a Truth that was crystal clear: 'Visions, powers, psychic gifts—they are passing clouds. Do not chase them. Do not cling to them. They are not the Truth. The true path is simplicity. Be still, be empty, be nobody.'

At first, his words were difficult to digest. After all the struggle, after all the nights of fire and fear, how could I accept that these extraordinary experiences were not the destination? The ego resisted and whispered to me, *Why would God give you such gifts if they were not important? Why would they arise if they were not meant to be cultivated and used?*

Yet, as I sat with this teaching, I gradually saw the Truth underlying Gautamji's words: Every vision faded. Every aura dissolved back into the ordinary. Every Tarot reading ended, leaving behind only silence. None of it lasted. None of it was permanent. What remained was not the visions, powers or the insights but the stillness—the silent ground of awareness that had been present before, during and after every experience.

Dilemma Dissolves

Even with this clarity, the inner battle was not over. The mind still longed for the extraordinary. It whispered of the sweetness of visions, of the thrill of being 'different'. Many nights, I sat torn between this enticement and the call to surrender the ego.

But whenever I returned to Gautamji's presence, the fascination weakened. His simplicity was the greatest teaching. He never paraded powers, never claimed specialness. In his quiet way, he lived what he spoke: humility, ordinariness and equanimity.

It was in this ordinariness that my illusions began to crumble. I saw that to cling to powers is to feed the ego and to inflate the very self—the 'I'—that must dissolve. True spirituality is not about becoming extraordinary; it is about realizing the extraordinary Truth of being nobody.

Kundalini's Master Plan

The powers did serve me, but not in the way I wanted them to. Now, when I look back on this period of powers, I do not see failure but the perfect play of Kundalini. I see that the Divine Mother had given these powers to me to expose my hidden pride. She first intoxicated me with them, then allowed the ego to rise again, only so that I could see its subtlety more clearly. She let me taste the sweetness of powers, only to reveal that they, too, leave the heart hungry. All this was done not to make me special but to show me how easily the ego can turn even the most sacred gifts into fuel for its perpetuation.

The powers were never the goal in themselves. They were tests. They were mirrors. They were illusions meant to be seen through. Gautamji's words, like a *mantra*, echoed in my heart: 'Be still, be empty, be nobody.'

And little by little, that stillness began to shine more brightly than any vision. That emptiness revealed itself as fullness, vaster than any power.

The lesson was profound: The only true treasure is surrendering the ego. Everything else, including bliss, visions and powers, is impermanent. The mind will chase them, but the heart will never be satisfied by them. Only when the ego is dissolved, only when one rests as nobody, does the peace that surpasses all understanding dawn.

4

Visions of Saints and the Dark Night of the Soul

The fires of Kundalini deepened, opening a new doorway before me. In dreams, in meditation and, sometimes, even in the stillness of the day, radiant beings appeared—saints, sages and masters, whose names I had only come across in books.

One night, Anandamayi Ma came to me, her presence suffused with a maternal love so vast that it made me weep. Her eyes were oceans of compassion, and her silence was like the embrace of the cosmos itself. On another occasion, I dreamt of Sai Baba of Shirdi, sitting quietly with his hand raised in blessing, his gaze dissolving every question in my heart. Once, in meditation, Sri Ramakrishna Paramahamsa appeared, his face luminous with bliss, whispering truths that seemed to bypass the mind and sink directly into the heart.

These were not vague impressions or the play of imagination. Each vision carried a strong fragrance, a power that shook me to my core.

When these saints appeared, the very atmosphere seemed charged, time seemed to stop and, in those moments, all fear vanished. It felt as though unseen hands were holding me, assuring me that I was not walking this path alone.

The Sweetness and the Snare

Waking from such visions, my heart overflowed with devotion. I felt blessed, chosen and carried by some of the awakened masters. The sweetness was intoxicating, a nectar that erased all sorrow for a while.

And yet, despite this grace, I was subtly falling prey to the ego. Without realizing it, I began to feel proud of these visions. A quiet voice whispered, *See how special you are. The saints themselves visit you. This is proof of your progress. This is a sign that you are destined for greatness.*

The ego, ever cunning, had returned once again to ensnare me and assert itself. Now, it wore the robes of devotion.

It was my guru's grace that exposed the ego's game. Gautamji, with his piercing clarity, told me plainly, 'Spirituality is not about being special. These visions are blessings, but they are not the Truth. If you cling to them, they will bind you. The path is not about being chosen but about dissolving into surrender.'

His words cut through the cloak of delusion. I saw how easily even divine visions could become food for the ego. The saints were not appearing to make me proud. They were reminding me to bow more deeply, to be grateful and to surrender.

Dark Night Descends

Not long after these visions, the sweetness receded, to be replaced by great emptiness. The saints appeared less often, until, eventually, they disappeared altogether. The bliss that had elevated me earlier was gone. The auras, insights and visions evaporated like mist in sunlight.

What remained was silence. But not the luminous silence of peace. It was a heavy, barren silence, empty of comfort, empty of joy. This was the descent into what mystics call 'the dark night of the soul'.

The nights became unbearable. Sleep fled. My body shook with restless energy, yet exhaustion weighed me down. My mind was filled with doubts: *Have I lost my way? Was the rising of Kundalini a mistake? Has the Divine abandoned me?*

At times, despair grew so strong that I wondered if life was worth living. The bliss had shown me heaven, but now I was trapped in a wilderness where even God felt absent.

Lessons of the Night

In those long hours of emptiness, I saw how attached I had become to experiences. Bliss, visions, powers and the company of saints had become my invisible crutches. And now that these experiences were gone, I felt stripped bare, left with nothing to lean on.

Only later did I understand that this was the purpose of the dark night. Just as Kundalini had burned away my illusions of control, it was now burning away even my attachment to God's nearness. Even the longing for bliss, the craving for visions and the need for assurance had to be surrendered. No illusions could remain.

The Mother was teaching me the most difficult lesson of all: Truth cannot be found in what comes and goes, no matter how divine it appears. Bliss appears and disappears. Visions appear and disappear. Even the felt sense of God's presence can appear and disappear. What remains when all these vanish, *that* alone is real.

The saving grace was that, gradually, a small beam of sunlight pierced through the clouds that had engulfed my soul. Though the bliss was gone, the visions had ceased and even God seemed absent, the substratum on which all this was happening still remained, unmoved. An awareness, silent and untouched, watching all of this unfold persisted.

This awareness did not offer comfort or ecstasy. It offered something deeper: stability. It was the ground that had always been there, whether the night was filled with visions or emptiness. It was not an experience but the space in which all experiences come and go.

Slowly, painfully, I came to see that even the dark night was not abandonment but an embrace. The saints had stepped aside, the bliss had withdrawn and the visions had vanished, so that I would not cling to them. All this, so that I could discover the formless presence that remains when everything else is stripped away.

From Darkness to Light

Now, when I look back at that spell of darkness, I see it as one of the greatest blessings of my journey. It was long, but it was not cruel. It was the Mother's most merciful teaching. She took away every crutch, every sweetness, every comfort, so that I would be forced to turn inward to the Truth that cannot be lost.

The saints had not abandoned me. They had only hidden their forms so that I would find the formless. The bliss had not betrayed me. It had only dissolved so that I would taste the peace that lies beyond it.

The dark night itself was not death. Rather, the new dawn which came in its wake was its death. A dawn whose eternal light stripped away all illusions, so that it could shine by itself.

5

Amrit, Aum and Endless Energy

After the dark night, the Divine Mother revealed yet another face, among Her many. This time, the experience was neither a blissful vision nor a barren emptiness. It was something more constant, more relentless than what I had experienced so far, as if She had decided to show me Her power directly, without veil or pause.

Nectar of the Gods

A sweetness, subtle at first, like the taste of watered-down honey, filled my mouth. Soon, this nectar grew stronger. It felt cool and had a flavour unlike any I had ever known in this world. It was neither food nor water; not even the sweetness of love. It was something altogether otherworldly.

The scriptures speak of *amrita*, the nectar of immortality. I had read those words with awe, but I never imagined tasting it. Now, as drops of this nectar seemed to flow into my throat unbidden, I felt it was a sign: Kundalini was opening realms that belonged not to imagination but to the deepest truths hidden in our being.

The taste would come at odd times: while sitting in silence, while walking down the street and, sometimes, even in the middle of a conversation. It was as if the Divine Mother was reminding me, gently but unmistakably, *I am with you, even in the ordinary moments. My grace flows within you, invisible yet real.*

Sound of Creation

Alongside this nectar came another extraordinary gift, which was the inner sound. Day and night, the sound of *Aum* resounded within me, not as something I chanted but as a vibration alive in the very fabric of my being.

It was as though the current of the Universe had found a voice inside me. Sometimes, it rang like temple bells, vast and clear. At other times, it was like distant thunder rolling through the chambers of my mind. Once, it became a hum, so deep that it seemed to shake each and every cell in my body.

This sound was unending; I could not switch it off. Whether I wanted it or not, it pulsed through me. And while it was magnificent, it was also overwhelming. I wondered how I could live an ordinary life when the sound of Creation was roaring through me.

Unstoppable Current

But the most challenging of all was the energy that poured ceaselessly through the crown of my head. At first, it felt like a blessing, a gentle fountain of light showering down on me. But soon, it grew stronger. The current became so intense that it never left. Twenty-four hours a day, it pulsed, surged, rose and fell, but it never ceased.

Headaches became constant. My skull felt as if it were being split open. At night, the current grew stronger, robbing me of sleep. My body trembled as though plugged into an unseen lightning bolt.

There was no pause, no rest, no escape.

I remember lying awake in the darkness, whispering to myself, *I cannot live like this. Either this current will kill me, or I will go mad.*

Descent into Desperation

In my desperation, I turned to books and unguided practices from the internet. I tried *spinal breathing*, *visualizations*, *mantra japa* and *chakra meditations*. I thought, perhaps, if I could 'direct' the energy, it would calm down.

But every attempt only made things worse. The headaches deepened, the insomnia grew unbearable, my digestion faltered and my mind frayed at the edges. Instead of peace, I felt more and more ungrounded.

At that time, I truly believed I was on the brink of collapse. My body was in turmoil, my mind was starting to fail and my daily life had become nearly impossible.

Lifeline of Guidance

It was then that grace appeared in an unexpected form. I came across a book, *Kundalini Diary: A Visual Journey in Meditation*, written by Santoshji, wherein she describes her own Kundalini journey—visions, images and phases of fire and sweetness. For the first time, I realized that what I was going through was not madness but a known passage, a sacred unfolding.

Later, in conversation with Gautamji, he reminded me

of the simplest truth: 'Stop trying to control. Surrender. The same force that awakened this current knows how to complete it. Your efforts only interfere. Let it move in its own wisdom.'

At first, these words seemed impossible to heed. *How can I not do something when the current is tearing me apart?* But slowly, I began to test his guidance. When the energy rose, instead of resisting, I breathed and let it flow. When the headaches came, instead of panicking, I accepted them as part of the cleansing.

And a quiet miracle unfolded. Though the current did not cease, my suffering lessened. The more I surrendered, the less unbearable it became.

Kundalini: A Double-Edged Sword

Through this experience, I learned Kundalini's greatest secret: It is never against us. It may be fierce, unrelenting, even terrifying, but its purpose is not destruction. It is purification. It strips away what is false, so that the Truth can shine.

The nectar, the sound of Aum, the ceaseless current—none of these were punishments or rewards. They were the Divine Mother's way of reshaping me, burning through every knot of resistance and pouring Her energy through every channel of my being until nothing false could remain.

It was not my place to manage or command Her but to bow, trust and surrender to Her.

Now, when I recall those long nights of headaches, those days of ceaseless vibration, I see them as blessings in disguise. Without them, I might never have learnt true surrender. Without them, I might still believe that spirituality is about control, about shaping the path according to my will.

The Mother taught me through fire that Her wisdom is beyond my mind, beyond my control. And Gautamji, with his steady guidance, showed me that the only true response is surrender.

This chapter of my journey reveals a truth I carry in my heart: Even when the current feels unstoppable, even when it strips away all comfort, it is still the Mother's grace. Her current is never chaos. It is a perfect order, leading us beyond the turbulence into the peace that cannot be shaken.

6

Confluence of Kundalini and Advaita

The Kundalini process is not something that can be explained to those who have not walked it. It is not a technique or a path you can choose; it is a force that chooses you. Once awakened, it moves at will, stripping away illusions, burning through shadows and shaking the very foundations of your identity.

For me, this journey became unimaginably intense. There were times when I felt I was being taken apart and remade every single day.

Out-of-Body Experiences (OBEs)

Often, without warning, I would find myself floating above my body, looking down upon it as if it belonged to someone else. The sense of separation was so real that I sometimes wondered if death had come. At other times, I felt myself shrinking into a point of awareness smaller than a seed, suspended in the vastness of space—a single dot of consciousness in an infinite void.

These out-of-body experiences were awe-inspiring but also terrifying. They dissolved the certainty of 'I am here, in this body' and revealed that Consciousness was not bound by form. And yet, as extraordinary as they were, they did not bring peace. When I returned to the body, fear often followed because I did not know how to live with such instability.

Body as an Instrument

Meanwhile, energy coursed through me twenty-four hours a day. My muscles twitched and jerked, as though they were strings being plucked in the instrument of my body. Sometimes, I would sit quietly, and my body would begin to sway or shake without my volition. It was as if the Divine Mother had taken possession of this instrument, playing out the music of purification in every nerve and cell. There were nights when the current was so strong that my entire body vibrated like a drum being struck by unseen hands. Other nights, I was awakened by surges so fierce I thought my heart would stop. Yet, in the midst of this storm, a hidden intelligence was at work. Slowly, I saw how old tensions in the body were dissolving and how deep knots of fear were being released through these movements.

Confronting the Past

Perhaps the most difficult phase was the flood of childhood memories that arose unbidden. Scenes I thought long forgotten returned with startling clarity: the sting of being mocked, the shame of being rejected, the loneliness of being misunderstood. These memories were not faint recollections; they were vivid, raw and alive, as though happening all over again.

At first, I resisted. *Why am I being dragged back into the past? Why reopen wounds that have already healed?* But the truth was they had not healed; they had only been buried. Kundalini was pulling them out of the subconscious, forcing me to face what I had hidden. Each memory that surfaced was a knot being untied, each wound a burden being lifted.

It was painful, but it was also cleansing. The Divine Mother was leaving nothing untouched.

'Doing' Becomes My Undoing

During these storms, I often made the mistake of interfering. I devoured books on Kundalini, eager to find methods that could 'help' the process. I experimented with breathing practices, visualizations and chakra manipulations. But each attempt only made things worse. The headaches grew more severe, the body pains more intense and the mind more ungrounded.

Only later did I realize the simple truth: Kundalini cannot be controlled. It is not an energy to be manipulated by the ego. It is the Divine Mother Herself, infinitely wiser than the human mind.

To interfere is to resist Her work. To try to command Her is arrogance. The more I tried to 'do', the more I suffered.

Marriage of Fire and Silence

Finally, only Gautamji's guidance of not trying to control the energy but surrendering to it saw me through this ordeal. It was here that the deeper Truth of Advaita began to shine. Kundalini is the fire. It stirs everything, brings every shadow to the surface and burns away all that is false. Advaita is the silence that does not interfere or control but simply points to the Awareness in which all this unfolds. At the very core, Kundalini is the Self. Shiva and Shakti are one.

When I combined the two, everything changed. Kundalini brought forth my wounds, my fears, my illusions. Advaita asked, *Who is it that suffers? Who is it that remembers? Who is it that feels bound?*

Again and again, the enquiry dissolved what Kundalini had exposed. The fire brought the impurities to light, and the silence of awareness dissolved them. Together, they became one process. The burning and the stillness. The storm and the sky.

This union became the bridge in my journey. The bridge from turbulence to surrender, from phenomena to the Self.

Living the Teaching

Now, when I look back at those storms, I see their hidden perfection. The out-of-body journeys showed me I am not the body. The flood of memories revealed the wounds that still bound me. The endless current taught me the futility of control. And, through it all, Advaita pointed me again and again to the ground of Awareness that had never been disturbed.

In daily life, this confluence of Kundalini and Advaita took simple forms. When anger rose, I watched it as a cloud passing. When in bliss, I enjoyed it without clinging. When fear returned, I breathed it out and let it dissolve. Slowly, my relationship with the process shifted from resistance to trust.

The goal was no longer to 'achieve' something or to accumulate experiences. The goal—if it could even be called a goal—was to remain as the witness, the silent awareness that is untouched by all that rises and falls.

And in that witnessing, I discovered something precious: a peace that was not dependent on bliss, not shaken by fear, not altered by visions. A peace deeper than experience itself.

7

Trusting the Current

The Kundalini current had now become a constant companion. It was no longer something that appeared only in meditation or rare moments. It surged through my body day and night—unrelenting, unpredictable and unstoppable.

Seized by the Current

I remember nights when I would be shaken awake, as if struck by lightning. My body vibrated violently, as though connected to a live wire. Three or four times, I experienced a force so intense that I thought I might combust into flames. My breath stopped, my heart stopped and my body burnt with energy.

Amid this storm, visions appeared. Radiant goddesses with blazing eyes, deities shimmering with power, and forms that appeared and vanished like lightning. Some seemed to offer blessings, others terrified me with their fierceness.

Earlier, I would have fought these experiences or clung to them in fascination. But now, Gautamji's words echoed in my heart: 'Allow it. Do not fear. Do not resist. Surrender.' They grounded me, and instead of panicking, I lay still, letting the energy move as it wished. Instead of questioning, I breathed deeply, to pacify the intensity of the force. Consequently, a quiet miracle unfolded: Though the current remained strong, my suffering lessened. The fire did not destroy me; instead, it purified me.

Anchored in the 'I Am'

Alongside these energy surges came a tide of traumatic dreams. Night after night, memories of childhood bullying, old humiliations and forgotten wounds replayed themselves. I would wake up in tears, exhausted by the ghosts that refused to leave.

Many times, I pleaded with Gautamji: 'I want these dreams to end.' His response, as always, was calm and piercing: 'Your very need for them to stop is what keeps them alive. Don't give them energy. Let them be.'

At first, I did not understand. *How could I simply let them be when they haunted me every night?* But slowly, I began to follow his advice. I stopped resisting. I stopped begging for them to disappear. I allowed them to rise and fall like waves.

And to my astonishment, the dreams began to loosen their grip. Their intensity softened. The more I stopped fighting them, the more they dissolved on their own.

During the day, too, Gautamji's teaching became my compass. He reminded me repeatedly, 'Remain as the 'I Am'. Stay as Awareness. Do not get lost in the play of experiences.'

So I began to practice this. When a surge of energy came, I watched it as a witness. When bliss appeared, I let it pass. When fear arose, I received it with the same stillness. Slowly, the mind began to settle. The body still shook, the current still roared, but inwardly, there was more space, more stability.

The shift was subtle but profound. I was no longer at the

mercy of the energy. I began to feel carried by it, as though the current itself was the hand of the Divine Mother, guiding me where I needed to go.

Mother's Reassuring Presence

Time and again, in the midst of fire, this simple yet powerful knowing would wash over me: *I am not alone or abandoned. The same power that awakened this process is the one sustaining it. The Mother has not left me; She is carrying me through.*

This knowing became a balm in my darkest nights. Even when I could not feel bliss, even when dreams dragged me into old wounds, even when visions terrified me, the silent reassurance remained: *You are not alone.*

Through this surrender, something remarkable happened. What once terrified me became bearable. What once felt like punishment revealed itself as purification. Every surge of energy, every traumatic dream, every restless night, was the Divine Mother's way of cleansing me.

The process was still fierce, but it was no longer hostile. Fear slowly transformed into reverence. Instead of asking, *Why me?* I began to whisper, *Thank You. Do with me as You will.*

Surrender Is Supreme

Now, I see those dreams and surges of energy as milestones of grace. The current did not come to destroy me but to dissolve my resistance. The dreams did not come to punish me but to free me from hidden wounds. The goddesses did not come to frighten me but to show me that the Divine is both sweet and fierce, both gentle and terrifying, and that to love Her is to embrace all Her faces.

Trusting the current was one of the hardest lessons I learnt. It demanded letting go of every instinct to control, fight or escape. But in that letting go, I discovered a truth that has never left me: Surrender is not weakness. Surrender is strength. It is the strength of trusting the Mother who knows the way.

8

Dance of Delight and Denial

From the very beginning of my spiritual journey, my heart belonged to the Divine Mother. She was not an abstract concept or a distant goddess. She was my constant refuge, my Beloved, the presence to whom I poured out all my prayers, tears and gratitude.

However, when Kundalini awakened, this devotion became visceral. It was no longer only words uttered in prayer or feelings stirred by *bhajans*. It was alive in my body, my breath and my very cells. The Divine Mother was not outside me; She was moving through me.

The Ecstasy of Her Touch

There were days when the nectar of bliss flooded me. Cool streams of energy poured through the crown of my head, spreading a sweetness that left me trembling with joy. Vibrations rippled across my skin, my heart throbbed with sacred fire and spontaneous tears of devotion streamed from my eyes.

Sometimes, the ecstasy was so overwhelming that I wanted to dance, sing or simply collapse at the Mother's feet in surrender. Each current of bliss felt like Her caress. Each wave of ecstasy was Her play. In those moments, I felt like a child held in the arms of its Mother—safe, loved and intoxicated with Her presence.

Delight Turns into Darkness

Yet, just as suddenly as it came, the sweetness would vanish. In its place came heavy waves of despair. There were periods when I sank into depression, so deep that even the will to pray felt futile. The same energy that once lifted me into rapture now dragged me into misery.

Dreams became dark and relentless, dredging up old wounds and traumas. My body ached with pains no doctor could explain. Sleep eluded me, leaving me restless and raw. Sometimes I would wake up with the sense that I had been pulled through centuries of grief in a single night. At other times, I cried out in complaint: *Why, Mother? Why give bliss only to snatch it away? Why intoxicate me with nectar, then plunge me into fire?*

The heart that once sang with devotion now ached with bitterness. I felt abandoned, punished and bewildered.

Embracing Her Unconditionally

It was Gautamji who patiently revealed the truth of these swings. With his compassion and clarity, he reminded me that my attitude was immature. 'You want the bliss and not the fire. But the Mother's grace is not partial. She comes as sweetness, and She comes as purification. To love Her truly is to embrace both.'

These words revealed to me how my devotion was mixed with demand. I was willing to love the Divine Mother only when She came as nectar but not when She came as flame. I revelled in Her grace when She gave ecstasy, but cursed Her when She gave pain.

This was not surrender. It was bargaining.

Slowly, through Gautamji's teaching, I began to bow to the Mother in Her entirety. When bliss arose, I received it as Her gift. When despair returned, I whispered, *This too is You, Mother. This too is grace.*

It was not easy. Many times, the mind still longed for the sweetness and rejected the shadows. But, little by little, I began to see the wisdom of embracing both. The bliss was not a reward. The despair was not a punishment. Both were Her ways of purifying me.

The Mother was not cruel. She was thorough. She wanted me whole, stripped of every illusion, freed of every clinging. To achieve that, She came in all forms—sometimes tender, sometimes fierce.

Grounded by the Guru's Wisdom

During this period, Gautamji's presence became a stabilizing force. His teachings reminded me that the play of bliss and despair belonged to the realm of experience. And all experiences, however exalted or terrible, come and go. 'Do not measure your progress by what you feel,' he told me. 'The measure is whether you can remain at peace in both sweetness and suffering. That peace is the true gift of the Divine.'

Gautamji's words taught me to see both ecstasy and agony as passing waves. What mattered was not the waves in the ocean but the ocean itself. The silent Awareness in which all experiences arise and disappear.

Now I see those alternating tides of nectar and darkness as the dance of the Divine. The Mother was teaching me that true devotion is not about clinging to pleasure or running from pain. It is embracing Her in all forms, both in bliss and in despair, in sweetness and in fire.

The nectar taught me to love Her. The darkness taught me to surrender to Her. Both were necessary. Both were grace. What once felt like a contradiction now feels like completeness. The Divine Mother is not only the soft caress of bliss but also the fierce flame of transformation. And to know Her truly is to embrace both, with gratitude, trust and surrender.

9

New Experiences, Same Ego

As Kundalini's work unfolded, the inner world became a theatre of extraordinary phenomena. It was as if the veil between the seen and the unseen had thinned, and a flood of experiences poured through.

Seduction of Being Extraordinary

There were nights when I saw people who had already passed from this world. They appeared in dreams, either asking for help or simply standing silently, their presence heavy with longing. Their faces were so vivid that, when I awoke, I could not dismiss them as mere imagination.

I also began to have visions of people I loved, often in states of distress. Once, I dreamt of my brother crying out in pain, clutching his knee. The dream shook me, and concerned, I called him the next day. To my astonishment, he told me he had fractured his knee the night before. On another occasion, a close friend who had longed for a child appeared in a dream, radiant and pregnant. Soon after this vision, she told me she was expecting.

These experiences seemed miraculous. They convinced me that Kundalini had opened avenues of perception that stretched far beyond ordinary boundaries.

Alongside these visions came synchronicities. Thoughts I carried would manifest in the outer world. Small things at first: thinking of someone and receiving their call subsequently or wishing for something and seeing it appear unexpectedly. Once, I was thinking of a childhood friend whose contact I had lost. Two days later, he called me out of nowhere. We had not been in touch for over a decade. I once wished for a pyrite stone and my friend gifted the same to me without knowing my fondness for crystals.

Over time, these synchronicities grew more striking. It was as if the Universe itself was responding to my inner states.

The ego, ever hungry, was quick to seize this. It goaded me on: *You have powers. You are becoming special. Your mind can shape reality itself.*

And so, without realizing it, I slipped once more into the trap of fascination. I found myself waiting eagerly for the next vision, the next synchronicity, the next proof of 'specialness'.

It was intoxicating, but it was also dangerous. For every moment of exhilaration, there followed a restlessness, a subtle hunger for more. The peace of the Self was forgotten in the chase for the extraordinary.

I later saw how cunning the ego can be. Even after being burnt by Kundalini's fire, even after being humbled by the dark night, it subtly returned, saying, *I am clairvoyant. I can heal. I can see what others cannot.* The same old pride, hidden under the mask of sacredness—making it even more dangerous than the ordinary everyday ego.

Guru's Intervention

At this critical juncture, the grace of my guru intervened again. Gautamji, with his steady presence, reminded me firmly, 'These are not signs of progress. They are distractions. Powers, visions, synchronicities—they are all part of the *Universal Mind*, not the Self. They may arise, but they are not the Truth. Do not cling to them. Do not measure yourself by them. Be still. Be nobody.'

At first, the ego protested: *How can such extraordinary things be meaningless?* But slowly, as his teaching sank in, I began to see clearly that none of these phenomena gave lasting peace. They arose, dazzled and passed away, leaving behind the same restless hunger.

They were not liberation. They were ornaments. And to mistake these ornaments for the gold (from which they are made) is the greatest delusion.

Freedom of Simplicity

Slowly, through Gautamji's guidance, I began to let go of the hunger for experiences. I still honoured them when they arose, but I no longer clung to them. I began to see them as clouds drifting across the sky. Beautiful, and even awe-inspiring at times. But transient.

The sky itself, the silent awareness in which the clouds appeared, was what mattered. That sky did not change, did not dazzle or demand attention. And yet, it was vast, steady and peaceful in a way no vision could ever be.

As my guru's teaching became increasingly self-evident, I saw that true freedom lies not in multiplying experiences but in transcending them altogether. Bliss and despair, visions and emptiness, and powers and powerlessness all belong to the realm of what comes and goes. What I am is the Awareness in which they arise and disappear.

Looking back upon those days of visions, powers and synchronicities, I see them not as failures but as necessary lessons. The Mother allowed me to taste them so that I could see their emptiness. She gave me glimpses of the extraordinary so that I would not cling to them but go beyond them. It was through them that I learnt the importance of simplicity, humility and surrender.

The Truth is not dazzling. It is quiet. It is not in the visions of saints or the powers of the mind. It is in the stillness of being nobody.

10

Health, Destiny and Acceptance

Even as the fire of Kundalini purified my inner world, my outer life began to bear the weight of the process. The body, which had carried me faithfully through years of ordinary living, now became the stage upon which the Mother's dance was performed. And it was not always a gentle dance.

Body Becomes a Burden

My headaches grew relentless. I felt a pressure in the skull as though the crown was being pried open. Sleep was fragile as it was often broken by sudden surges of energy. This left me exhausted in the mornings. My digestion weakened, my appetite waned and my strength diminished.

There were days when simple tasks felt overwhelming. A walk left me breathless. A meal left me unsettled. My body felt like a battlefield that was torn between its limitations and the power of an energy too intense for its frame.

Doctors could not explain what was happening. My test reports were normal, yet I knew something extraordinary was moving inside me. The challenge was not to find a cure but to endure, trust and surrender to what could not be explained.

Destiny Is Divine Will

My destiny was also something that I had to contend with. These questions kept knocking at my door repeatedly: *Why had this path chosen me? Why this upheaval, this turbulence, this unending fire?*

There were times I envied those who lived ordinary lives, unaware of the fire of Kundalini awakening. *So why was I different? Was my destiny a blessing or a curse?*

The mind compared, complained and questioned. But in the quietest moments, a deeper knowing held me gently: *This is your path, your destiny. You could not escape it even if you tried.*

And slowly, painfully, I began to see that destiny is not punishment. It is the precise unfolding of Divine Will. To resist it is to suffer. To surrender to it is to be free.

Teaching of Acceptance

Once again, Gautamji reminded me with clarity and compassion, 'The body will go through its own destiny. Do not measure your spiritual progress by its health. The body belongs to Nature. It will merge back into the five elements. However, the Self remains untouched.'

These words were like cool water poured over burning skin. They reminded me that my true identity is not this fragile frame and nor are the pains or the sleepless nights. The body is but a vehicle, and it will follow its destined course. It will be subject to extremes—strength and weakness, health and sickness—and will eventually perish. But the Self remains untouched, unbroken, ever free.

Acceptance became the teaching of this phase. Not passive resignation but active surrender.

When headaches came, I told myself, *This too is the Mother's grace.* When insomnia returned, I let the night be what it was, rather than spend my energy fighting it. When weakness weighed me down, I rested, honouring the limits of the body instead of resenting them.

And something beautiful unfolded. The suffering softened. Not because the symptoms vanished but because my resistance did. The pain was still there, but the bitterness was gone. In its place was a quiet trust: *Whatever the body must go through, let it be. I am not the body. I am the witness of its play.*

Alchemy of Suffering

What once felt like a burden slowly revealed itself as metamorphosis. The body's struggles were not meaningless. They were part of the Mother's way of softening my pride, humbling my ego and teaching me patience and compassion.

Each headache was a reminder of surrender. Each sleepless night was an invitation to rest in awareness. Each weakness became a lesson in humility.

I now see that my physical suffering, too, was an inseparable part of my awakening. It stripped me of illusions of control. It forced me to bow to destiny and to accept what I once thought unbearable.

The Mother uses even suffering as a tool of transformation. Nothing is wasted. Nothing is outside Her grace.

The body may weaken, the mind may tremble, but the Self remains radiant, untouched. This was the Truth Gautamji pointed me to, again and again. And as I began to live this Truth, the struggle transformed into gratitude.

11

Flowering of Love and Devotion

After years of fire, visions, despair and storms of energy, something within me began to soften. It was as though the fierce work of Kundalini had cleared enough space within me for a gentler fragrance to now arise from the heart. The sharp edges of struggle melted into tenderness, and what once felt like a battle slowly began to feel like an embrace.

Floodgates of the Heart Break Open

I found myself weeping often, not out of sorrow but from a welling-up of love that had no object. Simple things stirred tears: the sight of sunlight falling on leaves, the sound of children laughing and even the stillness of an empty room. My heart overflowed, unable to contain the immensity of feeling that arose without cause.

Sometimes, the love directed itself towards the Divine Mother. I would find myself whispering Her name, my body bowing without thought, my chest swelling with devotion. At other times, it flowed outward towards people, animals and the Earth itself. It did not discriminate, it did not choose. It gushed out of me, like a river overflowing its banks.

From Fire to Nectar

The currents of Kundalini, once fierce and overwhelming, began to carry a different quality. Instead of burning, they soothed. Instead of shaking me up, they caressed. Energy still surged, but it moved with a sweetness, filling me with waves of *bhakti* rather than fear.

There were days when I felt intoxicated with love. My body swayed spontaneously, as if dancing to music that only the heart could hear. My lips whispered prayers without effort. Even silence itself seemed filled with devotion.

The same energy that once terrified me now filled me as nectar. The Mother who had come as fire now revealed Herself as tenderness.

In this phase, I no longer longed for visions or powers. I no longer chased after bliss or feared despair. What mattered was simple: to love, to surrender, to bow.

Bhakti: The Path, Not the Destination

I discovered that true bhakti has nothing to do with effort. It is not about chanting or rituals. It arises naturally when the heart is emptied of its clutter. Just as fragrance emanates from a flower without force, devotion arises from a purified heart without effort.

Sometimes, the love was directed to form: to the Mother, to the guru and to God (in names and images). At other times, it dissolved into formlessness, a love so vast that it had no direction, no object and no end.

In this flowering, Gautamji's presence illuminated the path. He reminded me gently that even devotion, though beautiful, belongs to the play of duality. 'The love you feel is sacred,' he said, 'but do not cling even to that. Bhakti is the bridge, not the destination. Let devotion flower fully, but let it also dissolve into the stillness of what you are.'

These words left me deeply impacted. I saw that devotion itself, as intoxicating as it was, was another wave rising in the ocean of Awareness. To cling to it would be to remain bound. To let it flow freely, without attachment, was to be carried to the shore of silence.

Love as Surrender

Over time, I began to see that love and surrender are not separate. True love is surrender. When the heart bows fully, when it offers itself without condition, that is devotion. And that devotion is nothing but the recognition that life is not mine, that I am not the doer and that everything belongs to the Beloved.

This understanding transformed my relationship with life. The struggles of the body, the storms of energy, the rise and fall of moods—all were embraced as expressions of the same Beloved. There was no longer a need to reject anything. Love received it all.

In retrospect, I see this flowering of devotion as the natural ripening of surrender. The fire of Kundalini had burned away my illusions and my pride. The dark night had stripped me of false comforts. And in that emptiness, love arose, not as something I created but as something that simply revealed itself. This love was not personal; it did not belong to me. It was the fragrance of the Divine moving through an emptied heart.

The flowering of devotion taught me that the path is not about becoming extraordinary. It is about becoming simple, tender, permeable and surrendered. When the heart is emptied of the self—the 'I',—love flows naturally, and *that* love itself is grace.

12

Naturalness, Stillness, Ordinariness

There comes a point in the spiritual journey when all striving falls away. The fires of Kundalini burn through the body-mind. The storms of visions rise and fade. The sweetness of devotion blossoms and dissolves. And what remains is neither ecstasy nor despair, neither effort nor renunciation. What remains is simplicity.

No Destination

For many years, I was consumed by the idea of progress. The mind wanted milestones: powers, visions, bliss, union and, ultimately, realization. Each time something extraordinary arose, I believed I was closer to the goal. Each time it faded, I feared I had lost my way.

But slowly, through the fire of Kundalini and the grace of Gautamji, I began to see the Truth: There is no progress. There is no goal ahead. The Self, what I truly am, is not something to be attained because it is ever-existing.

The very notion of a 'path' dissolves. There is only life—rising, falling, flowing—in the silence of Awareness.

Natural Flow

In the natural state, nothing is forced, nothing is resisted. The body breathes, the heart beats and thoughts may come and go, but there is no interference, no clinging. Life lives itself.

Ordinary actions, once dismissed as mundane, now shine with quiet radiance. Drinking a glass of water, walking across a room, exchanging a smile with a stranger—all are suffused with the same stillness. Nothing needs to be extraordinary, for the essence of life is already complete.

Meditation is no longer sought as a separate practice. Life itself is meditation. The silence that appears only in samadhi, flows through waking, walking, speaking and resting.

Serenity

In the natural state of our being, the mind loses its compulsive restlessness. Thoughts may still arise, but they no longer bind. They are like birds passing across the sky—brief and harmless, leaving the vastness untouched.

Earlier, I wrestled with the mind, trying to meditate it into silence. Now, stillness is relatively effortless. It is not the absence of thought; it is the absence of identification with thought. The mind may move, but the Self remains unmoved.

This stillness is alive; it is vibrant. It is not dull or passive. It is a luminous peace that holds everything without judgement.

Miracle of Everyday Living

Contrary to what one may imagine, the natural state is ordinariness. After years of chasing mystical experiences, I expected myself to be in a constant state of dazzling ecstasy. But the Truth is the opposite: it is utterly ordinary.

Life continues; the body eats, sleeps, works and laughs. There is no halo, no sense of being 'special'. In fact, the very idea of being special has vanished. What freedom there is in this ordinariness! To no longer need to be extraordinary. To simply be what *is*. This is peace that pervades our daily being.

As Gautamji often reminded me, 'The spiritual process is not about becoming something more. It is about becoming nobody.' Now I understand that to be nobody is the greatest joy.

Living in Naturalness

The natural state is not something to be achieved. It is not the result of effort. It is the fruit of surrender, ripened by grace.

Kundalini settles. The energy rests in silence. Devotion continues, not as a demand or an intoxication but simply as a fragrance of gratitude.

In the natural state, nothing is gained, nothing is lost. The ego dissolves, and life flows effortlessly. Actions happen, words are spoken, love arises and challenges appear, but it all happens without a doer. Everything belongs to the Beloved.

This is freedom. It is not an ecstasy or an escape from life but life itself, lived with simple, unshakable peace.

Looking Back

I now see the wisdom of every stage of my Kundalini journey. The bliss that awakened trust. The fire that purified me. The visions that exposed the ego. The dark night that stripped me bare. The devotion that softened my heart. And finally, the stillness that is the Truth.

Each stage was the Mother's way of bringing me home. Each step was necessary, even when it felt unbearable. And in the end, I see that the journey was never mine. It was always Her work, Her play and Her grace.

What remains is gratitude. Gratitude for the fire, gratitude for the darkness, gratitude for the guru and gratitude for the Beloved who revealed Herself as what I always was.

This is the natural state. The end of seeking, the end of struggle, the end of becoming. The simplicity of being. The peace that has no opposite. The ordinariness that is divine.

13

Integration: Living Advaita in Daily Life

Awakening is often imagined as the end of life's story—a final escape from the world, a vanishing into silence. But, in truth, awakening does not take us away from life. It brings us more fully into it. Once the fire of Kundalini has burnt away the illusions and Advaita has revealed the Self, life continues. Simple, ordinary, radiant.

No Separation Between Inner and Outer

For years, I divided my existence into two dimensions: 'spiritual' and 'worldly'. Meditation was sacred, relationships were mundane. Visions were divine, and daily chores were distractions. But in the natural state, this division vanished.

Now, cooking a meal, speaking with a friend or sweeping the floor carries the same stillness as sitting in meditation. Silence is no longer limited to the cushion or the retreat hall. It breathes through the whole of life. There is no 'inner world of spirituality' and 'outer world of activity'. All is the same flow, the same play of Consciousness.

Daily Life: The Ground of Spiritual Practice

Perhaps the greatest transformation has been in my relationships. Earlier, I longed for blissful states but avoided the discomfort of daily interactions. When old wounds were triggered by family or friends, I ran back to meditation, trying to escape into silence.

But Gautamji taught me that true spirituality must be lived in relationships. If one's interactions are filled with conflict, superiority or avoidance, then awakening has not been integrated into daily life.

Slowly, I began to bring awareness into my closest bonds. When pain from childhood memories resurfaced, I learnt not to resist. Instead, I saw them as opportunities for healing. When old resentments towards my parents arose, Gautamji reminded me, 'See God in them too. To see divinity only in visions is easy. To see it in your parents, in those who trigger you—that is maturity.'

This teaching softened me. I stopped demanding love from others and, instead, let love flow through me, without expectation. Forgiveness, once impossible, became natural. Compassion replaced judgement. In this way, relationships became the real temple of practice, where awareness, humility and surrender were lived and not just spoken of.

My work, too, underwent a gradual transformation. Earlier, I often carried tension about achievements, reputation or results. Now, seeing clearly that I am not the doer and that everything unfolds by Divine Will, actions happen without the burden of *doership*.

Whether the task is small or large, whether the outcome is success or failure, the peace remains. Life unfolds, and it is witnessed in gratitude. However, this does not mean passivity.

Actions still happen. Responsibilities are still carried out. But they are no longer stained with pride or guilt. They are simply the functioning of life through this body-mind instrument.

I see why the sages often appear so simple. Awakening does not make one grand; it makes one natural. There is no need to appear special, no desire to impress. The miracle is life itself, lived moment to moment, free of burden.

Guru's Invaluable Role

As this integration unfolds, my gratitude to Gautamji only deepens. His guidance keeps me grounded, his presence dissolves my illusions and his teachings bring me again and again to simplicity.

Without him, I would have remained lost in visions and powers, chasing phenomena and mistaking them for Truth. With him, I learnt to rest in what does not come and go.

His greatest gift was not his answers but the living demonstration of Advaita in daily life. In his ordinariness, in his kindness to all—whether a waiter, a rickshaw driver or a student—I saw the real face of realization.

Living Advaita

Living the teachings means that there is no more inner war, resistance, ownership or doership. Life is as it is. The river flows, and I flow with it. This is Advaita made flesh. It is not a philosophy but a way of Being.

And in this, the Kundalini journey finds its fruition. The fire, the visions and the storms were never the end. They were preparations. They were the Mother's way of burning me clean, until only simplicity remained.

Looking Ahead

Integration is not an achievement. It is simply life lived without division. The natural state breathes through daily tasks, relationships, work and rest. The guru's guidance continues as an inner compass, reminding me to stay in surrender.

And now, the journey feels less like a path and more like a homecoming. Nothing to reach, nothing to become—just the grace of Being, lived in every breath.

This is the essence of integration: not to escape the world, but to live fully in it, with the heart anchored in silence. And also, this is the paradox of integration: to be nobody and, in that, to be everything.

PART II

ODES TO THE DIVINE MOTHER

The Poetry of Devotion and Surrender to the Divine Mother

When words could no longer hold my experiences, when the storms of Kundalini dissolved into silence and when the Advaitic Truth began to shine, something unexpected began to arise: poetry.

The poems in Part II are not the result of effort or intellect. They poured out spontaneously, in moments of ecstasy and in hours of despair, in devotion and in surrender. They were not crafted by the mind but gifted by the Heart—sometimes through whispers or tears, and at other times, through fire. The poems burst forth as cries from the depths of darkness and also as songs of gratitude and love.

Looking back, it is evident to me that the poems chart the same path that the chapters in Part 1 of this book trace: from the turbulence of Kundalini awakening and the fires of purification to the sweetness of surrender and the simplicity of the natural state. They are the fragrance arising from the preceding prose and are not separate from it. I pray that these poems touch you not as explanations but as invitations—to feel, to surrender and to rest in the same silence from which they were born.

These poems are the story of a soul's relationship with the Divine Mother. They are Her voice speaking through the cracks of my brokenness as well as silence echoing through words. They are born from the fire of Kundalini, the sweetness of surrender and the struggles of ego meeting grace. To read them is to walk alongside me through the storms and the stillness, the nights of anguish and the mornings of rapture.

At their heart, my poems convey three movements of the spiritual journey:

1. **Longing and Confession**
   Many of these verses come from the raw cry of the heart. They speak of pain, rejection, betrayal and the feeling of being a misfit in this world. Yet, within that human suffering, there is a deeper yearning—the longing to be embraced by the Mother. In these cries, I reveal the helplessness of the child who knows there is no refuge in the world; only She is the saving grace.

2. **Purification and Fire**
   The Mother does not merely comfort; She transforms. You will encounter images of burning, of storms, of being shattered and being restored. This is Her power as She rises, stripping away every false identity, every illusion of control. It is not always gentle. It is fierce, relentless, like lightning in the spine or fire in the heart. Yet, even in this pain, there is hidden sweetness because the fire purifies, heralding Her blessing in its wake.

3. **Union and Surrender**
   Beyond longing and purification lies the mystery of union. Some of the poems sing of bliss, of intoxicating nectar, of unbroken music within. They speak of a love that does not come and go, a presence that pervades every cell, every

breath. This is the heart of surrender—not the end of life but the fullness of it. In this state, the Mother is no longer outside but revealed as the very Self, the very being of the devotee.

Through these movements, my poetry conveys a living testimony: that the Divine Mother is both fierce and tender, destroyer and nurturer, song and silence. She is not an idea or a doctrine but a living presence who enters the life of the devotee and overturns everything.

These poems are also a mirror. They are not only about my journey; they are meant to awaken something in you, the reader. Perhaps, you will recognize your own longing, struggles and glimpses of grace. Maybe, these words will remind you that the Divine is closer than your breath, waiting for your surrender.

The journey with Kundalini, the Divine Mother, is not one of comfort. It is the marriage of fire and sweetness. She burns the false and fills the heart with nectar. She wounds the ego and heals the soul. She brings both tears and laughter, despair and bliss, until all that remains is surrender. I cannot claim these poems as mine. They belong to Her.

If you find beauty in these lines, it is Her beauty. If they stir something in your heart, it is Her call that you are hearing. May these poems remind you that the Mother is alive, waiting in your own heart, and may you have the courage to surrender to Her grace.

Note: The poems that follow are written by one who has undergone the Kundalini journey and not by an established poet. Hence, they should be read as the honest outpourings of a soul who has emerged from the experience and not as works of refined literature.

THE AWAKENING OF FIRE

1

The Mother's Fire

You roasted me like the meat on the barbecue.
Felt like a rebirth from the ashes of fire, it's true.
I felt so resurrected and fresh—anew!
Initially, it seemed like being caught
in a perilous quagmire too.

Now, this scorching heat and blazing bliss
feel like the Mother Divine's embrace and kiss,
dousing the suicidal and deep illusion.
Surrender is the only solution.

2

Lightning in the Spine

When you finally arrived,
it was lightning
striking with all its might.

To others, this encounter may
seem contrived.
In that spiritual explosion,
surrender happened—
there was simply no
resistance or fight.

You rose up the chimney of
the spine;
with all your might
you popped each petal like popcorn.
What sublime delight!

3

The Divine Storm

In the heart of bliss, I Am;
even beyond that, I Am.
I Am in the fragrance of the rose,
interwoven in spiritual poetry and prose.

And even beyond that, I Am;
I am very near and yet very far.
I am in every form,
yet beyond the form.

I am divinely destructive
in my Kali aspect,
disrupting every single falsity and norm.

Invite me into your heart.
I will destroy everything false
with my divine storm.

4

The Rose and the Thorn

A rose blooms in my heart,
a serpent coils along its stem.

Pain and beauty entwined,
every petal sings your name,
every thorn reminds me of your power.

5

Currents of Fire

Currents surge through spine and bone;
each vibration whispers,
I'm not alone.

I burn, yet cool,
I laugh, yet cry,
Mother, in your arms, I fly.

6

The Serpent's Hiss

Mother, you have dissolved my turbulent emotions.
You are soothing my being with your divine lotion.
There is peace amidst commotion.

The train of thought has halted.
The energy towards the crown has risen;
I am jolted.

The empty void is suffused with intoxicating bliss;
this is the most exquisite serpent's hiss.

7

Silvery Ascent

If you accept me as your child,
every suffering shall become mild.

If you so will,
please go wild;
make me still.
Your grace shall take me uphill.

If you choose to rise
through the spine to the top,
then, without shattering everything,
you simply don't stop.

As the silvery snake ascends
the spinal tube,
I melt in my devotion,
like a sugar cube.

8

Divine Alchemy

She rose—an unstoppable fire.
It was like burning alive
on a funeral pyre.

She shattered all my false conditioning
that had been constantly hardwired.

I cried, wailed, resisted;
but eventually, I surrendered,
unfolded.

Recognition dawned:
She alone was in control,
while I, an innocent child,
proceeded blindfolded.

In that sweet surrender
occurred the divine alchemy—
the union of the Beloved
and my soul.

THE DARK NIGHT AND THE SURRENDER

9

From Darkness to Light

I thought it would be bliss, all light and fun,
unaware that from my fears and trauma,
I could not run.

You shook my being
with the dark night of the soul,
unimaginable pain—
a heart with a gaping hole.

Yet, through the alchemy of surrender,
the hole became the Whole.
If the energy body is unprepared,
the fire can be intense,
and the frailness of the body
may pay the expense.

So, do not hurry,
do not strive;
simply yearn for love,
simply be alive.

Drop the heavy burden
of a spiritual goal;
sip your tea, breathe,
and let life console.

See the Divine Mother
in each step, in every tree,
as you wander through Nature,
in her grace, free.

10

From Ashes to Bliss

She dropped me into a bottomless pit.
At first, my faith took a hit.
With my inner demons, I began to sit,
as surrender unfolded, bit by bit.

She raised me from the fiery ashes,
every illusion like an apple she mashes.
Every identification and attachment she slashes.
Sometimes, her energy is so intense,
the skin erupts in itches and rashes.

In her raw potency, she makes you surrender each pretence;
she breaks through the illusion, which is dense.

If you chase powers,
she will blast your life's towers.

But if you let her enter your heart
in utter surrender,
unimaginable bliss she showers.
Mother Divine is the most loving and tender.

11

Cry for Grace

I crave your love every moment.
Don't abandon me;
this is utter torment.

I cry buckets of tears,
realizing that at your feet,
I must surrender all my fears.

The conditioning is so thick,
stacked up in many layers.
Polish me in all aspects and spheres.
Burn me in your holy fires.
Crush me under your heavy, grace-filled tyres.

Let the union take place.
Let me behold you in every face.
I wail and cry for your grace.
Save me from getting caught up
in the world's materialistic race.

12

Anchor in the Infinite

In this world of changing appearances,
you are my only support and anchor.
After these worldly pleasures,
I don't care to hanker.

I keep craving your divine presence and light.
You embody the brilliance of ten thousand suns—
it's the most exquisite, blinding, lightless light.
Raise me to the greatest spiritual height.

In that ascent, don't forget to burn
every trace of 'me' and 'mine'.

13

Pathless Path

As I have drowned in your love,
I don't know whether I am male or female.
Where have you taken me to sail?
This is a pathless path,
where no one has left a trail.
I don't know who I am
or from where I hail.
Sometimes, your bliss makes me red;
at other times, pale.

This path is akin
to being crucified with nails.
Only those ferry across,
whom you so wish,
and who, on the altar of Truth,
lay their life.

14

Heart Ablaze

My heart ignites with every beat,
pain and joy in flames do meet.
Consumed by fire, yet rising free,
laughing in your ecstasy.

15

Graceful Stride

I thought the journey to meet you
would be all fun and a ride.
But I had to learn to take
all life situations gracefully
in my stride.

In this awakening journey,
there is nowhere to hide.
Forever grateful I am,
that in you,
every joy and sorrow
I can confide.

For this blissful union,
every worldly activity
can fall by the wayside.

16

Where Gentle and Fierce Meet

Seeing you in both your forms,
you gave me the strength
to break through
illusions and false norms.

One aspect, ever so gentle;
yet another, so fierce.
From the inception, every illusion
they begin to pierce.

You are the nectar
in the mouth.
In the same breath,
you are blissful yet terrifying,
emerging from the south.

Only the devotee who
embraces both your flavours,
he alone experiences;
ultimate bliss he savours.
That true devotee asks for no favours.

17

Your Shelter

Mother, take me into your gentle shelter;
else like a dead leaf, I shall fade and falter.

If I am the fish, you are the flowing stream.
If I am the bird, you are my endless dream.
Lose you, and life itself would cease.
In your embrace alone, I find my peace.

Other than you, all else is naught—
nothing matters, nothing is sought.
You are the ocean, the sky, the flame,
all that is, forever calls your name.

18

The Silent Ocean

I drown within your silent sea;
and in that depth,
you speak to me.

Every wave, a sacred song;
in your vast arms, I do belong.

19

Divine Dance

You possessed the totality of my being.
There is simple, pure seeing.
As you raged through my every pore like a vibratory fire,
It felt like an ecstatic burning at the funeral pyre.

Like a roast chicken in the oven,
I feel charred and baked.
You bared my heart naked.

The dance endlessly happened, and the dancer disappeared;
for my sanity, everyone feared.
As I wait for sleep,
you call from recesses deep.

When you blaze my entirety,
even insomnia is not a problem,
although it may last for an eternity.

THE PLAY OF THE MOTHER

20

Nectar of the Divine

As the tongue folds
back to the roof above,
a nectar descends—
a gift of love.
It trickles softly,
drop by drop;
a stream of bliss,
it does not stop.

It nourishes deeply,
the body and soul;
it lifts the spirit,
it makes me whole.
I ride on waves
of sweet elation,
lost in endless adoration.

Each cell lights up,
a radiant flame;
ecstasy sings the Mother's name.

I fall in love,
again and again;
with boundless joy,
beyond all pain.

21

Mystic Wine

O Mother, take away my worldly lust,
lest for an eternity, I shall rust.

Deprive me of sex and worldly pleasure,
but bestow upon me thy precious treasure.

The worldly wine intoxicates me not,
it just makes my liver rot.

Sip by sip, your mystic wine
dissolves the illusions
of 'me' and 'mine'.

Your love is the greatest orgasm;
with your nectar,
fill my heart's chasm.

You run the whole universe.
To describe or fathom your greatness
fails every scriptural verse.

22

Celestial Flute

You turned the spine
into a mystic flute,
burning away all
I felt was 'me' and 'mine'.

In my heart, you took root.
As you rose,
I wrote poetry and prose.

Unbroken celestial music would play,
as you ascended
and made your way.

Fire of love in the heart,
only you could start.

Tears would flow,
yearning would grow.
My heart's desire
you would always know.

At your lotus feet,
with reverence,
I eternally bow my head.

23

Only Your Love Is Priceless

On a hot sunny day,
my head is dancing
with a cool current.

While on a winter night,
I feel so hot,
as if the heat
will make me rot.

Laughing in pain,
crying in joy.

In your love,
I cry and whine
as you lift me
into raptures sublime.

Eyes keep flickering in joy.
I am your ignoramus,
your foolish boy.

Psychic abilities and siddhis
are like a useless toy.
Everything is useless;
only your love is priceless.

24

To Merge with the Beloved

Occultists foolishly think
they can make you a slave;
they do egoic chanting
next to the grave.

When power is the goal,
The result will be
a cancerous mole.

In delusion, there is never
emergence of the Whole.

To merge with the Beloved,
you have to surrender
your doership and desire.
Only then, your heart
is set on fire.

25

Sweet Surrender

How can I hate anyone,
when you pervade everyone?

Wherever I look and see,
your vision sets me free.

You are the Creator
and the Creation.
People fail to see your glory
in their frustration.
Feeling you viscerally
is an ineffable sensation.

The surrender is the sweetest;
bogus is the egoic manifestation.

Nothing sweeter
than childlike trust;
to merge in Mother's innocence
is a must.

26

Child of the Mother

Like a child, I run to your side.
Innocence melts my foolish pride.
You are the ocean—vast, unknown;
yet in my heart, you are my home.

No mantra, no ritual, could ever be
as sweet as resting inside thee,
O Mother, Kundalini flame.

27

Where Are You?

Mother, why do you hide from me?
I search in the temple,
I search in the tree.
I call your name
with a trembling voice,
But you are silent,
and I have no choice.

Are you playing a game
with your child?
Smiling at me, unseen,
all the while?
Sometimes, you show me
a glimpse, a spark;
then you leave me alone
to confront the dark.

O Mother, without you,
food has no taste.
Without your touch,
this life is a waste.

Take away pride,
take away will;
Make me child-like,
innocent, still.

You are the fire,
you are the flame.
You are the One
who takes all the blame.
Even my cries
are yours, not mine;
Mother, all is your play divine.

So hold me close
in your lap today;
prevent your little child
from running astray.
In laughter or tears,
in silence or song,
O Mother, in you I belong.

Forever I burn in your holy name.

28

O Virgin Mother

Gentle Mother, pure and bright,
you shine with Heaven's holy light.
Through your heart flows endless grace,
tender love upon your face.

In your gaze is mercy's flame,
compassion flows through, all the same.
You hear the cries, the silent tears,
you calm the hearts weighed down by fears.

Virgin Mother, guide my way;
keep me near you, night and day.
When I stumble, when I fall,
lift me with your tender call.

O Mother Mary, humble, true,
my soul finds refuge only in you.
Through every trial, joy and strife,
you are the light that fills my life.

29

When the Water Breaks

Mother, when the water breaks,
life is born.
So too from the navel
your light is torn.
It spreads through my body,
it fills every place,
with joy, with bliss,
with your embrace.

From head to toe,
the currents flow.
Each chakra shines,
begins to glow.
My heart is dancing,
my breath is free.
O Mother, you are all to me.

You break the shell,
illusions fall.
I see your hand
behind it all.
O Mother of love,
O ocean wide,
in your arms I rest,
in you I abide.

30

Mischievous Mother

O Mother, you are so mischievous and naughty.
You never let your devotee
grow proud or haughty.

You open the Pandora's box
of karmic tendencies;
you shatter all delusions
and fantasies.

The ego-driven go mad
and crazy.
You never let anyone
grow complacent or lazy.
Yet, you are always caringly
lurking around,
making sure your devotee
is finally free
and not bound.

THE DEVOTEE'S UNION

31

She Roars in Her Glory

She roars in her divine glory,
shattering every victim story.
She walks you through
every transient satori.

She transports you
to realms unknown.
With her grace,
divine seeds of bliss
she has sown.
With surrender,
they have sprouted and grown.

Countless are the spiritual realms.
With her intensity,
even saints she overwhelms.

No spiritual mystic
can know her fully.
She is a mystery, infinite and inexplicable—truly.

32

Beloved Mother's Ocean

My parents wish to see me
married to a worldly bride.
But this secret,
how can I hide?
I am already in love
with Mother Divine;
even in pain and infamy,
everything seems fine.

How will I love
that worldly bride,
when my gaze
will be transfixed upon you,
who are always by my side?
This undeniable truth,
in whom shall I confide?

In your love,
and fearing separation,
I wail and cry;
so how can I attempt
this transient societal tie?

Why don't my well-wishers
understand my heartfelt emotion:
This worldly union
could lead to
an irrevocable commotion

Now that this divine play
has been set
in perpetual motion.
It will never end,
even after immersing
in my Beloved Mother's ocean.

33

The Final Prize

Many think it is the end
when the mystical union
happens in the head.
Few know that after the rise,
in the cave of the Heart
lies the final prize.

At the crown,
the void is at the start;
but as you descend
into the bosom,
that's the final spring
and blossom.

Now, what unfolds endlessly
is an unsolved mystery—
one that has never
made it to
the pages of history.

34

Everlasting Flame

I wept, I pleaded, I tore apart,
I opened wide the door of my heart.
Then Mother came—not dream, not sight,
but burning Presence, fierce with light.

She hollowed my bones
and filled with gold,
a nectar sweeter
than your imagination
will ever behold.
Now, waking or sleeping,
by night or by day,
her pulse is my rhythm,
to it I endlessly sway.

O Kundalini,
O Mother Divine,
your fire eternal
is now wholly mine.
No passing joy,
no fleeting game,
but endless union,
an everlasting flame.

35

Eternity to Eternity

You have set me on divine fire.
Take me with you even higher.
I really love you, Divine Mother;
I promise, I am not a liar.

I want you to love me
from eternity to eternity.
I say this with absolute certainty.
Even if this love
leads me to insanity,
let me sacrifice myself
for humanity.

36

At the Altar of Eternal Truth

As I watch all things slip away,
no resistance and pain remain.
Disowning all pleasure and gain,
I release all anxiety and strain.

At the altar of eternal Truth,
this life has been lain.

37

Blazed by the Glory Divine

I yearned for only
sweetness in my life,
but all it gave was
betrayal and strife.

Rejected by this transient world,
I found sweet solace;
I received unconditional love
from Mother Divine's face.

By her grace,
I drank the mystic wine;
even in struggle and suffering,
everything was blissful, all was fine.

She burnt away everything
I thought was 'me' and 'mine'.
Destroying the transient,
she blazed me
with her glory divine.

38

Fiery Bliss, Mysterious Rain

Foolish are the ones
who think they can control you.
Only love and surrender are true.

Yoga postures and pranayamas,
they budge you not.
In devotional intoxication,
you roar like a boiling pot.
You make my muscles twitch;
my hands and feet,
they burn so hot.

As you course through my veins,
taking hold of life's reins,
an electrifying bliss
you kindle in my brain.

It's the most mysterious rain
you pour from above.
You rise from below
like a white dove.

Fiery bliss seems like
being grilled on a hot stove.

When it overwhelms me,
foolishly, I sometimes resist.
But as you play
hide and seek,
I crave for you, my Beloved;
I want your love
to eternally persist.

39

Beloved Without a Second

Mother,
you appear as the play
of countless forms.
Yet, truth be told,
you are One,
not manifold.

The seer and the seen,
the lover and the loved—
all dissolve
in your silence.

I called you, Mother,
but in that calling,
the caller vanished.

No hands to hold,
no heart to yearn;
only stillness—
your vast, unbroken face.

The fire, the river, the sky;
the breath rising and falling,
all whisper, I Am That.

O Mother,
you are not outside,
nor inside;
you are the very space
where both dissolve.

In this empty fullness,
the game of devotion ends.
Yet, Love remains—
without an object,
without a name.

40

At Your Divine Feet

Life rests surrendered
at your divine feet.
Love flows endlessly
as my false self burns
with your divine heat.

For lifetimes, I yearned
to merge and meet.
Whatever you bestow
is nectar sweet.
I rest all my worries
at your feet.

In my heart,
you have taken
an eternal seat.

My love for you is endless;
yours is manifold—boundless.

In that love, I disappear,
from eternity to eternity.
You are always here.

41

Homecoming

She coils no more, she rules the flame;
the throne of my heart bears her name.

The river dissolves in the ocean's embrace;
no shore remains, no time, no space.

No rise, no fall, just silence deep;
the mind has vanished into sleep.
The crown is hers, her reign is true;
no 'I' remains—there's only you.

Mother Divine, you took it all—
the house, the sky, the cosmic hall.

Only you, O endless friend;
Only union without end.

42

The Serpent's Kiss

She rose from the root, a secret flame,
untying the knots, erasing my name.
Like snow, I melted in her embrace.
She crowned my head with lightning's grace.

One kiss from her, and all was undone;
no path of return, no place to run.
She breathes in my breath, she thinks in my thought,
she lives in the stillness the sages sought.

No state, no seeking, no fleeting bliss.
I am her marrow, her skin, her kiss.
She is my Being, my soul, my breath—
union unbroken, beyond all death.

MANIFESTATIONS OF THE MOTHER

43

Always by My Side

Currents up and down the form,
like an unstoppable storm;
in cold winters, feel extremely warm.

Trapped among snakes,
exploding buildings and raging fires.
Getting betrayed by worldly liars.
Sometimes, feeling small
as a mustard seed;
other times, humongous,
like a wild weed.

Sometimes, I feel inside,
at other times, outside.
This mystery,
in whom should I confide?
This process,
I need to hide,
No doctor would understand
far and wide.

All I know is
Divine Mother Kundalini
is always by my side.

44

Hide and Seek

O Mother, why do
you play hide and seek?
People think I am
an eccentric freak.

Sometimes, a blazing fire
in the heart.
At other times, an enlivening,
cool current in the crown—
in each and every part.

People search for this joy
in megamarts.
Nobody knows it's within
since the very start.

45

Strange Are Her Ways

Blinding colourful lights,
even when the room is dark.
The fear is intense,
as if I will be devoured
by a wild shark.

Smelling roses
when there are none.
Seeing blazing lights
when there is no sun.

At times, birds chirp
and music plays.
Strange are
Mother Kundalini's ways.

Sometimes, it's all bliss and fun.
Often, in this process,
from fears, I can seldom run.

Sweet surrender is the mystical key,
allowing oneself to drown
in this unknown sea.
It will eventually set you free.

46

Her Glorious Face

The cooling breeze upon the head.
In the mouth, a nectarine bliss is fed.
Seeing auras with open eyes,
piercing through illusions and lies.

I am like a battered pomfret
whom Mother Kundalini fries.
Nobody can control her,
no matter how hard he tries.
She sees through all pretences and lies.

She breaks unnecessary ties,
strips your illusions bare
to dissolve every hidden fear.

Bow to her grace,
if you wish to behold
her glorious face.
It's not an egoic race.
In revealing herself,
She removes your egoic trace.

47

Your Intoxicating Current

How ethereal and divine
are you, Mother!
In your love,
I see no other.

For everyone
I was a weird misfit.
Everything changed
when your arrow of love hit.
I danced in intoxication
and just could not sit.

Time faded,
and your bliss pervaded.
At every juncture of life,
your grace aided.

Complex are these
worldly relations.
Difficult are these
mundane conversations.

Only your love is worth seeking.
Though hiding in your devotee's life,
you are always peeping.
And once you choose,
in every pore of his being,
your intoxicating current is seeping.

48

Mother's Grace

To be in my Mother's embrace,
every illusion
I have to face.

Every trauma
must be seen as a drama.
Only then
can I behold my Divine Mama.

The head
has to undergo birthing pains;
only then can come
the divine gains.

You show all the scenery
on the spiritual train;
no moment or experience
is unholy or profane.

Very few
reach the destination.

Some, deluded by ego,
alight at the wrong station.

They chase psychic abilities,
which eventually lead
to delusion and disabilities.

Nothing is sweeter
than the Mother's lap.
Power, lust and money
are the biggest trap.

49

Quantum Leap of Faith

When you rose to the height,
every illusion vanished
from my sight.

The brain short-circuited
with currents so sublime
that I lost all sense of time.
Joyous I became
without reason or rhyme.

You were drilling
and pecking at my skull
like a woodpecker does.
Into my brain descended
an electrical buzz
and fuzz.

Sometimes, I felt
as if I would combust.
But your grace
made me robust.

This is a journey
of blind trust.
A quantum leap of faith
is a must.

50

The Journey Within

As you reached the navel,
all hidden emotions
began to unravel.

As you ascended
to the heart,
grudges dissolved
and unconditional love
began to start.

As you hopped to the throat,
removing blockages
took a long time;
but eventually, what came forth
was poetry so sublime.

As you reached the point between the eyes,
you bestowed insight
and the ability to see beyond
all illusions and lies.

As you drilled through the skull,
terrifying was the void,
which the ego could not avoid.

When surrender unfolded,
the cave of the Heart
was renewed and mystically moulded.

51

In the Hush of Dawn

In the hush of dawn, your currents rise;
a silver serpent weaving through my sighs.
Shadows melt where your light descends.
Every broken corner of my heart you mend.

The world dissolves in your tender flame:
Names and forms vanish; only love remains.
I tremble in bliss I cannot name;
yet, in that trembling, I call your name.
Through every breath, your mystery flows,
and in your silence, my soul truly knows.

PART III

GRATITUDE TO THE GURU

Poetry of Thanksgiving and Love for the Guru

The poems in Part III are outpourings of an inner journey—a journey of longing, surrender and grace. They arose in moments of silence, in the fire of love for the guru and in the depths of spiritual transformation. Each poem is a reflection of the soul's dialogue with the Divine, the struggles with the ego, the pain of separation and the joy of union.

They are written for seekers—those who question the illusions of the world, who thirst for the Truth beyond appearances and who are willing to look within. Whether you are walking the path of devotion or self-enquiry, or simply yearning for peace, these poems may serve as mirrors, reminding you of the glory that already resides within.

The poems convey a simple yet profound message: Realization is not to be found in distant places or grand practices but in the grace of surrender, the dissolution of 'me' and 'mine', the embrace of divine love, and the silent presence of the guru. They speak of transformation, not through effort alone but through grace—an unseen hand that lifts the soul beyond suffering into freedom.

If you approach these poems with an open heart, you may find they do not just speak *to* you but awaken something *in* you. May they inspire you to trust the inner voice, recognize the divine fragrance within and discover the eternal flame that never dies.

Note: The poems that follow are written by one who has undergone the Kundalini journey and not by an established poet. Hence, they should be read as the honest outpourings of a soul who has emerged from the experience and not as works of refined literature.

THE LIVING MASTER

1

The Glory Within

I was so desperate to get transcendence.
There was nothing to attain but only
the loss of wrong concepts and ignorance.

Kept chasing you in pilgrimages and retreats outside;
all the while, you were waiting inside.

When you revealed yourself in all your glory,
it was the end of my victim story.

2

The Seer and the Seen

Getting obsessed with the physical body
is a pursuit so futile and shoddy.

This transient world is illusory and gaudy.
When you see the mirror,
see the ashes and not the impermanent body.

Investigate who is the seer,
then everything shall be crystal clear.

Truth is eternally here.
Drop all your resistance and fear.
Dissolution of the ego is the end of terror.

Don't look far for what you seek;
it is ever so near.

3

The Inner Voice

There is the divine inner voice
which is always guiding.
In ignorance and illusion,
we are resisting and fighting.

The more you block it,
the less your mind can sit.
With this approach,
how will the inner light
ever be lit?

4

The Fire of Divine Love

Breathing up and down the spine,
but not going beyond the delusions of 'me' and 'mine'.

Practise an indefinite spiritual fast;
know that this doership shall not last.

Only bathing in the holy rivers
shall not end your fears and quivers.

Contorting and twisting your body in a yoga posture
shall not give you ultimate composure.

Love and grace alone shall liberate;
all delusions, the fire of love shall obliterate.

This message, eternally I reiterate.

5

The First Glance

In the first meeting,
I implored you to heal this body,
which is nothing but ash.

Foolishly, I treated your holy feet
like garbage, like trash.

I thought I could buy your grace
with donations and cash.

You healed me, totally
and completely removed
the I-am-the-body belief.
It was the ultimate relief.

6

The Mysterious Meeting

The ignorant think that
they find the teacher,
but without the guru's grace
helpless is every creature.

With his grace, he finds
the rightful seekers.

In his tutelage, the student
becomes humble and meeker.

The mystic is the giver
of ultimate bliss.
It is the most exquisite kiss.

WORK OF GRACE

7

The Pain of Longing

I burn in misery when I can't meet my spiritual teacher.
He embodies every divine virtue and feature.

Every worldly pleasure can depart;
it shall not affect my heart.
But if you leave my life,
I'll self-immolate myself in endless strife.
I will rip my veins with a knife.
Scold and slap me, but set me free.

Never remove me from your divine sight;
it is like falling from the greatest height.

8

The Gift of Grace

I didn't do any penance,
yet was blessed with divine fragrance.

The guru took me spiritually high.
In his radiant heat,
I glowed like a firefly.

You can never figure it out,
no matter how much you try.
Realization happens only by grace;
it removes me and the mind's every trace.

9

Right Perception

I cried to you and asked,
'Why do these dreams last?
Please remove them fast.'

You told me to drop resistance,
but the ego fuelled their persistence.

As I embraced life in every aspect,
there emerged for you
a deep respect.

Situations were not causing confusion.
Right perception was the solution.

10

Sweet Nectar

I drink the sweetest nectar
as I look into your eyes.
Time simply flies.

You bestow wisdom
for life's every sector.

Your home is my only temple.
Over my unshakable faith,
none can trample.

Your holy feet are my
abode and refuge.

Celebrating life dispassionately,
I am no more a recluse.

11

Burnt Illusions

As your grace descended,
the illusion was transcended.

Your touch set 'me' into flames,
ending all self-perpetuating games.

You revealed the One
behind all forms and names.

12

Potion of Love

I am awestruck to see the love you exude.
You are verily God, I can easily conclude.

To every instruction of yours
I shall surrender.

Gratitude flows for you every moment.
Love is the ultimate potion,
ending all suffering and torment.

13

The Gaze Shifted

All along, I was chasing Truth
in the wrong direction.

In your love began intoxication.
Your wisdom bestowed divine perfection.

The gaze shifted from the object,
as I abided as the subject.

14

Loss Is Gain

In the dentist's chair,
I transcended all fears.

When he was messing up the operation,
you were by my side in that situation.

In that surrender,
I lost my tooth
but gained the ever-present Truth.

15

The Eternal Flame

You kindled in the heart
an eternal flame.

You removed pride and guilt,
destroyed my shame.

You showed that
you and I,
we are the same.

You stripped the habit of
condemnation and blame.

With your grace and guidance,
my destructive vices
I could tame.

16

Your Loving Embrace

Carry me in your loving embrace.
Imbue me with your
infinite love and grace.

Give me strength and wisdom,
so that my inner demons
I may face.

Raise me to the divine kingdom.
Your guidance is the portal
to ultimate freedom.

17

Grace in the Shadows

As I landed in realms
dark and occult,
you saved me from
a perilous result.

I got foolish, enamoured with
divination and powers;
you saved me with your
grace-filled showers.

Dangers still stealthily lurk,
but your grace can move mountains
and shake towers.

ONENESS AND COMPLETION

18

Childlike Innocence

Only if you could see,
trust and faith alone set you free.

Doubt and cynicism are a poison.
Haste and arrogance indeed a prison.

Only with childlike innocence,
to the kingdom of heaven has one risen.

19

Beyond the Mortal Frame

Your words took me to a space
that was beyond words.

As I lost myself in your eyes,
I saw a realm beyond paradise.

You took me beyond the mortal frame,
as we defeated and conquered
this illusory game.

20

A Unique Realm

You shone light on my path,
consecrated my being with a spiritual bath.

Taking me beyond dualities,
you removed the sting of striking polarities.

A realm so unique—
where there was no good or bad;
beyond the feeling of being
happy or sad.
I am forever your ignorant lad.

21

The True Treasure

When I was chasing pleasure,
you showed me the way:
'Inside is the true treasure.'

When the seeker and seeking disappeared,
the ever-present Truth appeared.

22

Endless Laughter

On New Year's dawn
the world turned still;
my guru's glance
broke every will.

A touch of grace,
a lightning spark,
lit up the soul,
erased the dark.

Laughter unbound,
three hours flowed;
no thought remained,
no burden showed.

Blissed out, aflame, my ego burnt;
in that moment,
I was reborn.
The ever-present Truth
was unearthed.

23

Love Protects

You drove the car,
as I wondered,
looking at the night star.

Throughout the tough terrain,
your love protected.
I always felt
it gave more security
than the seat belt.

As we reached, I realized
there was nothing to gain.
In that moment,
at the altar of Truth,
this life was lain.

24

The True Refuge

Everyone in the world
can backstab and betray,
but you will always have my back
and show me the way.

You burnt my useless book stack.
Your love kick-started
the internal dive.

This world is a stinging beehive.
With your love and light,
now I feel fully alive.

25

Your Divine Abode

As I entered your abode,
I saw a living Goddess.
Awestruck was I with your
spiritual prowess.

I felt naked and vulnerable,
fully I confess.

You showed me how the mind
was deluded and terrible.

As you taught me meditation—
the sovereign key;
that guidance set me free.

26

Mystical Presence

Everyone says formless alone is true,
but how can I say that to you?

The guru's form is reverential and holy;
to negate it is the biggest folly.

The form exudes a divine fragrance;
his divine aura is the door to transcendence.

His eyes are an ocean;
the words he utters, a divine potion.

His touch is alchemical;
his presence, ever so mystical.

27

Divine Perfection

Whenever I disobeyed your instruction,
I walked the path of self-destruction.

Your guidance was the portal
to divine perfection.

You explained scriptures,
section by section,
and then told me to drop
this intellectual dissection.

You are a father who sets me free.
I feel protected in your presence—
the shade of the evergreen tree.

BOND OF UNCONDITIONAL LOVE

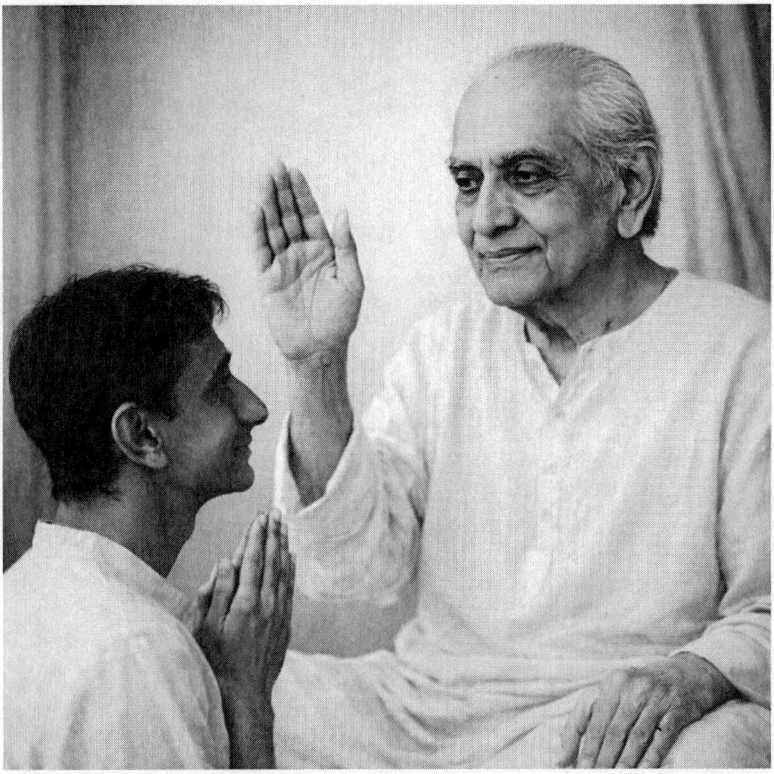

28

Melting at Your Feet

As you gaze at my third eye,
you burn every trace of 'me' and 'my'.

Your piercing gaze sees through my facade;
your transmission kindles a blissful cascade.

I burn in love when I am physically distant.
You burn the ignorance of seekers in an instant.

The one who surrenders at your feet,
his ego-death is imminent.

29

Where the Petals Unfurl

As I tune into your radiant aura,
for me, it reveals more than the Torah.

I see the emanation of the Goddess,
tempered with Advaitic prowess.

Your field brings stability
to people's Kundalini process.

You never make any spiritual claim;
you avoid public recognition and fame.

You lie low like a precious pearl.
In your presence, the petals unfurl.

30

The Nectar After the Fire

As I meditated in your presence,
I sensed fragrance in incense's absence.

Waves of bliss took over the room.
How can ignorance persist and loom?

Transmissions and releases happened at your feet;
the blessed prasad was a sumptuous, vibratory treat.

A thousand suns arose in that moment,
ameliorating years of suffering and torment.

Nectar pervaded following the recession of heat.
I bow at your feet for your remarkable feat.

31

Grace-Filled Rain

You told me to drop my self-pity.
You are always peaceful and witty.
You never expected a penny.

You embraced me with your bliss-filled heart,
as we sipped coffee and had Himalayan tart.

Trust developed, and surrender began to start.

In one moment, you joked about romance to a teenager;
in the next, your heart melted for a labourer.

As you walked people through the mountainous terrain,
with your compassion, you eased their pain.

Everybody reminisces about that grace-filled rain.

32

A Bond Etched in Eternity

Your sojourns, I often can't attend and travel,
but with your astral grace,
mysteries unfold and unravel.
Chakras are cleansed of their blockages,
just like dirty gravel.

We are separated only geographically;
Yet, through many lives,
we are connected historically.

I am certain you will patiently wait
as I drop greed, malice and hate.

Then we shall dance from eternity to eternity,
and this bond shall be etched in love for posterity.

33

Monk Without Robes

You are a wise monk without the robes;
people are unaware of your spiritual treasure troves.

Even sages dote on you because of your simplicity.
You never speak highly of yourself—
this is pure spiritual humility.

Always embodying childlike innocence,
you have experienced transcendence.

Always open and innocent, everything you endure;
it only shows your divinity and a heart so pure.

For the ignorant's malady,
You have a suitable cure.

PART IV

A ROAD MAP FOR THE KUNDALINI JOURNEY

1

Classic Signs of Kundalini Awakening

A Kundalini awakening can bring a wide range of physical, emotional, mental and spiritual experiences. These are natural signs of the energy's movement and should not be feared. Many seekers report the following experiences, although all of these will probably not occur for everyone.

- ❖ **Heightened Emotions**
    - Amplification of emotions, brought to the surface by the energy.
    - Intense rising of waves of joy, sadness, fear or anger.
    - Surfacing of emotions so that they can be seen, accepted and, ultimately, transcended. Until the unnecessary or detrimental belief systems and emotions are cleansed, Kundalini keeps bringing them to the surface.

- ❖ **Increased Sensitivity**
    - Enhanced perception of subtle energies in people, places and situations.

- Ability to sense someone's energy upon entering a room, shaking hands with them or meeting them intimately.
- Perception of auras or luminous fields around beings and objects.

❖ **Dreams, Visions and Subtle Realms**

- Vivid, symbolic or prophetic dreams.
- Inner visions during meditation or sleep, revealing guidance or truths.
- Spontaneous glimpses of past lives or karmic impressions.

❖ **Altered States of Consciousness**

- Natural and spontaneous absorption into states of samadhi during meditation.
- Spontaneous questioning of the self and reality: *Who am I? Where am I?* I would often come out of meditation confused about who I was and where I was in the house. Reorientation would happen after a few seconds.
- Awareness across the states of waking, dreaming and deep sleep. This is beautifully elucidated as the lofty state of *Turiya* in the *Mandukya Upanishad.*
- Temporary memory lapses where the past feels unreal or distant. For a phase in my journey, I lost memory of some parts of my childhood and often lost my train of thought. This is not something to fear as they are transient phenomena along the way.

❖ **Out-of-Body Experiences and Subtle Phenomena**

- Lucid dreaming and astral experiences. At times, I had dreams where I was flying and could control and re-enter the dream or subtle realms after waking up temporarily.

- Out-of-body experiences or the feeling of floating above the body. At times, I would wake up in the corner of the room or above my body. Re-entry into the body would be accompanied by a jolt and a strange sensation, difficult to describe to someone who has not had an OBE.
- Hearing subtle inner *nada* (sounds), such as bells, flutes or buzzing.
- Tasting amrita (subtle inner nectar) flowing into the mouth. At one point, it was trickling down my throat throughout the day. The taste is indescribable, but the closest I can relate it to is a mixture of sweet coconut water and honey.

❖ Spontaneous Physical Manifestations and Yogic Phenomena

- Spontaneous muscle twitches, jerks or shivering.
- Intense heat or cooling sensations rising through the chakras.
- Gentle swaying or circling of the torso.
- Sudden spontaneous *yoga asanas* (postures).
- Spontaneous *pranayama* (breath control) and *hasta mudras* (hand gestures).
- Unfamiliar but natural body movements during meditation or rest, such as spontaneous gentle rocking, spinal adjustments, or head rotation.
- All these spontaneous happenings are called *kriyas* in the *Shaktipat* tradition.

❖ Emotional and Devotional Expressions

- Spontaneous laughter or crying without apparent reason. Once, after listening to a devotional song, I laughed uncontrollably and continuously for three hours. On another occasion, I cried incessantly for hours as I sat with a deep feeling of gratitude for my guru. These, too, are spontaneous kriyas.
- Waves of devotion, bhakti or deep longing for the Divine.
- Ecstatic responses to music, chanting or sacred sounds.

❖ Other Classic Signs

- Pressure or tingling sensation at the Sahasrara Chakra. At one point, I was feeling a blockage at the nape of my neck. Later, after reading about it, I discovered that it is called the *Rudra Granthi*. As long as that constriction remained, energy would rise on the outer surface of the skull, accompanied by intense bliss. I felt tingling and sparking sensations over there. Eventually, the experience faded as the energy entered the brain, and I felt my entire brain being rewired by the energy.
- Feeling of energy moving like currents, spirals or lightning within the spine. At one point, I felt a long snake rising in the spine and merging into the brain. This was quite a visceral Kundalini experience.
- Sudden illumination, or an inner light, seen with closed eyes. Often, I would wake up to check whether the room lights were on or if dawn had arrived.
- Profound silence of the mind, or blissful absorption.

- A sense of the heart expanding with unconditional love. I could feel the sensation of unconditional love arise, sometimes accompanied by a fiery heat in the heart, and, at other times, by a cool, blissful sensation, as if a bucket of cold water had been poured over my chest. These experiences were often accompanied by devotional moods, tears and states of trance.
- Detachment from body and ego, glimpses of oneness, or the experience of void-like stillness in the advanced stages of Kundalini awakening.
- Waves of bliss or ecstasy throughout the body.

2

Pitfalls on the Path

While sailing across the ocean of Kundalini, it helps if one knows how to navigate the waters. There are some hazards that one must be wary of to make the voyage as smooth as possible:

- **Fear of Symptoms**
  The signs signify purification, not illness. Fear only adds resistance. So try not to give in to it.

- **Suppression of Spontaneous Movements**
  Allow kriyas, *mudra*s or swaying to happen, as long as they are safe and do not harm the body. Avoid suppressing these phenomena with medications or numbing methods, such as psychedelic drugs, as they can block the flow of energy.

- **Chasing Experiences and Clinging to Them**
  It is unwise to chase and get attached to mystical experiences, visions or blissful states as they strengthen the ego. They come and go, but realization itself is beyond them. Stay rooted in awareness and stillness.

❖ **Excessive Isolation**
Balance solitude with a healthy relationship with family, friends and community to stay grounded.

❖ **Neglecting the Body**
Eat nourishing food, sleep adequately and take care of physical health.

❖ **Overindulgence in Practices**
Excessive practice of pranayama, asanas, mudras or energy techniques without proper guidance can create an imbalance; so, moderation and the support of a realized guide are important.

❖ **Self-Diagnosis of Medical Issues**
If in doubt, seek medical support alongside spiritual guidance. Every symptom need not be characteristic of Kundalini awakening. It is important to remain discerning and grounded.

At one point, an acquaintance of mine believed she was experiencing subtle inner sounds, but it turned out to be tinnitus caused by an acoustic neuroma, a small tumour pressing on the ear nerve. In another case, someone dismissed chest pain, assuming it was the Heart Chakra opening, while, in reality, they were suffering from chronic heart disease.

True wisdom is knowing when it's time to seek medical help. Dismissing serious symptoms as purely spiritual can be risky. Spiritual practice and medical care are not in conflict; both can support and nurture life when approached with balance and discernment.

- **Walking the Path Alone**
  Seek guidance from a realized spiritual teacher or a trustworthy mentor. It would help to be part of a supportive community, if possible, where members could share their experiences and comfort each other.

- **Egoistic Approach to Kundalini**
  Do not chase Kundalini awakening for a sense of spiritual adventure, thrill or achievement. It is not entertainment but transformation. Also, feeding the ego's sense of being 'special' or 'chosen' only strengthens identification and delays surrender. Kundalini can lead you to liberation if you surrender, or turn you into an ego-maniac if you chase powers. It all depends on your inner attitude.

- **Trying to Force It**
  Forcing or trying to awaken Kundalini through extreme practices is unwise. The energy awakens by grace, not by force.

- **Drugs**
  Experimenting with psychedelic drugs in the hope of awakening the energy is risky and can destabilize the body and mind. They can tear open the *subtle body* prematurely, disturbing the natural rhythm of Kundalini awakening.

- **Imbalanced Approach**
  Projecting fears or desires onto visions, sounds or sensations is not helpful. It is better to see them as passing phenomena and not truths.

- **Sexual Extremes**
  Either overindulgence or rigid suppression of sexual activity can disturb the natural flow of energy. Balance is desirable.

- **Toxic Environments**
  Staying too long in negative company can be unsettling as sensitivity heightens during awakening.

- **Unrealistic Expectations**
  Expecting the journey to follow personal plans or timelines can lead to frustration. The awakening has its own divine rhythm.

- **Lack of Faith**
  Losing trust in the process makes the dark phases heavier. It is worth remembering that even the most intense struggles eventually give way to peace when surrender deepens.

Kundalini awakening is a sacred unfolding of life energy. It may bring intensity, beauty and challenge. However, when you surrender to it with faith, balance and humility, it ultimately leads to clarity, freedom and the realization of the Self.

3

How Does Kundalini Get Activated?

There are various ways in which Kundalini can awaken. Kundalini Yoga is practised with the express intention of arousing the Serpent Power. However, besides this, certain practices trigger Kundalini naturally as part of the process of spiritual awakening. Also, there are certain conditions that trigger it purely by accident. Given below are typical examples of the last two phenomena.

- ❖ Shaktipat, or energy transmission from a guru, saint or spiritual adept. It is like one flame lighting another.
- ❖ Prayer, devotion and sincere seeking of the Truth with devotion to God or through service to mankind.
- ❖ Yogic techniques:
  - Trataka, or concentrating one's attention on a single point, such as a candle flame in my case. (This is first on the list as it triggered my Kundalini awakening.)
  - Pranayama practice, such as *Kapalabhati* and *Bhastrika*.
  - Mudras and *bandhas*, such as *Khechari Mudra* and *Mula Bandha*.
  - Meditation, mantra japa and deep states of absorption.
  - Asanas practised with intensity and focus.
- ❖ Past-life spiritual practices or unfinished awakening carried forward into this life, resulting in spontaneous Kundalini awakening.

- Healing modalities, such as *Reiki* and *Pranic Healing* (both giving and receiving).
- Practice of *prana* (vital energy)-based martial arts systems, such as *Tai Chi* or *Qigong*.
- Listening to sacred mantras, devotional music or entering power-spots, such as *Jeeva Samadhis* of *siddhas*, *Shakti Peethas*, *Jyotirlingas* and temples.
- Intense *tapas* (austerity) that burns away conditioning.
- Intense concentration or self-enquiry (*Who am I?*) leading to inner silence.
- A sudden mystical epiphany, sometimes triggered by a book, scripture, vision or *satsang*. One of Santosh Ma's disciples experienced Kundalini awakening after reading her works on Kundalini, which included the images she had drawn spontaneously during her own Kundalini process.
- An upward (instead of outward) flow of strongly-activated prana through emotional intimacy or intense sexual intercourse. If someone's Kundalini is awakened, it can sometimes spark its awakening in their sexual partner. The process, however, can be intense, so awareness and guidance are important.
- Use of drugs, especially psychedelic ones. (These are very often destabilizing and hence their consumption is not recommended).
- Trance-inducing activities with heavy *pranic* overtones, such as ecstatic dancing, drumming, rituals and prolonged fasting.
- Childbirth, during which life-force energy surges through the system.

4

Importance of a Kundalini-Completed Guru

The necessity of a guru who has emerged enlightened from their Kundalini journey cannot be expressed in words, yet it becomes undeniable the moment one finds oneself in the thick of the Kundalini process. Kundalini is not an idea to be studied in books or a philosophy to be debated. It is a living fire that shakes the body, mind and emotions, often in ways that feel unbearable. When that force begins to move, it does not stop for theories or concepts. At such times, only someone who has already walked through the storms, been broken open by the fire and finally emerged into stillness can offer the kind of support and reassurance that truly helps.

I am blessed that Gautamji has been such a guide for me. He carries within him the wisdom of Advaita, which always points to the constant—the stillness beyond all experiences—and at the same time, he has the lived experience of Kundalini as it unfolded, more gently and gracefully for him than for many others. He has also witnessed first-hand the blossoming of his mother's Kundalini journey from start to completion, which gives him an intimate familiarity with the unpredictable phases and symptoms that arise.

There were times when I was overwhelmed by doubts and questions. Once, during a Zoom session with Gautamji and his mother, who herself is a Kundalini master, I asked whether the ringing sound in my ears during meditation was simply tinnitus or whether it was the subtle inner sound described in the scriptures. With great simplicity and authority, Santosh Ma clarified that it was indeed the subtle current of sound and not a medical problem, and Gautamji gently seconded her explanation. This cleared a deep confusion in me and lifted the heavy burden of fear. It showed me in a very practical way how precious it is to have access to those who have walked the path.

As sincere and competent as teachers from the *Bhakti*, Vedanta, Buddhist, Christian and Muslim traditions may be, the reality is that only a master who has completed the Kundalini journey knows the terrain: the sudden turns, the pitfalls that catch seekers unaware and the subtle illusions that the ego creates along the way.

If you are in the midst of a Kundalini awakening, having such a guide is not a luxury but an essential support. It is the difference between drowning in confusion and despair, and learning to walk through the storms with trust and surrender. One does not need another teacher who merely offers weekend courses on Kundalini Yoga or the scriptures, however well-intentioned they may be. What is needed is the steady hand of a guru who has lived it, who has walked through the darkness, and who now stands in the light, able to point the way with both compassion and clarity.

5

Frequently Asked Questions

The Nature and Purpose of Kundalini

What is Kundalini, and what does it do?

Kundalini is concentrated Consciousness. It is the living current of the Self. When it awakens, the movement begins through the physical, subtle and *causal bodies. Vasanas* (old tendencies) and *samskaras* (deeper impressions) rise to the surface to be faced and released. The body, mind and emotions are all purified on this journey.

Guided by Gautamji, I discovered from my own path that although the process shakes the physical form deeply, its purpose doesn't concern the body at all. Kundalini rises to bring about the dissolution of the ego, which is the return to the formless, pure Awareness that is untouched by anything. As the energy rises through the different layers, one experiences many visions, powers and phenomena, but all of them are the play of the mind. The true completion comes when the movement rests in the Spiritual Heart, and the ego-thought, the 'I', falls away. Then, there is only Consciousness Itself—still, radiant and one without a second.

What kind of *siddhis* (powers) does Kundalini awakening give rise to?

On my journey, I experienced certain powers and subtle gifts, such as visions, intuitive insights and even the ability to sense people's emotions. At first, they felt extraordinary. But I was constantly grounded by Gautamji's reminder: 'Do not cling to them. They are only clouds passing by.'

Siddhis come and go. To hold on to them is to feed the ego with ideas of superiority. Many seekers get trapped here, mistaking phenomena for realization. True spirituality has nothing to do with being 'special'. It is about becoming nobody; being simple, ordinary and free. If a teacher boasts of siddhis, it is a sure sign of delusion. The real path is surrender, not power.

Importance of the Guru on the Path

Why do seekers say that being in the physical presence of a true guru is important in the Kundalini process?

Kundalini, being unpredictable, can intoxicate you with bliss one day and throw you into terror the next. The body shakes, the mind doubts, the ego clings and, without guidance, many seekers lose their balance. In such a situation, the guru's presence is like an anchor in the storm. In its stillness, your turbulence begins to settle. In its ordinariness, your illusions of 'specialness' dissolve. The nervous system unconsciously aligns to the guru's calm field. This is not theory; it is living transmission.

There were nights when I thought I would go mad or die. But sitting with Gautamji, even in silence, settled the turbulence. My body became calm, the energy cooled down and the mind became quiet. Nothing was 'done'. It was his presence that held me when I could not hold myself.

How does continuous contact with a guru help, compared to just reading books or watching videos?

Books can inspire, and teachings can point to the Truth. But the awakened current needs continuous contact with a living guru to guide you to overcome obstacles, such as pride, when powers arise; despair, when darkness comes; and clinging, when bliss intoxicates.

Kundalini tests in subtle ways. Without the guru's timely reminder, 'Do not cling; do not resist; surrender,' the seeker can easily fall into delusion. The guru corrects these deviations in real time, keeping the process steady.

Each time I was swept away—by visions, despair or strange phenomena—I was steadied by Gautamji's words: 'These are passing clouds. Remain as Awareness.' Without that, I might still be lost in experiences.

What is the role of the guru's physical touch or *darshan* in the Kundalini process?

Physical darshan (simply sitting before the guru) or the touch of a guru can transmit a stabilizing force. It is not magic but alignment. Just as a candle flame lights another candle, the guru's grounded energy settles the disciple's turbulent current.

I have felt this directly. In Gautamji's company, the fiery surges became bearable, sometimes even sweet. In his presence, what was tearing me apart (when I was on my own) became part of a larger rhythm, a natural unfolding.

Does this mean one cannot awaken or complete Kundalini without a guru's presence?

Kundalini may awaken without a guru. But stabilization and completion—especially the descent into the Spiritual Heart—almost always require guidance. The Mother can be fierce. Without someone who has walked the fire and come through, the seeker may mistake visions for the Truth, powers for realization and despair for failure.

A true guru does not give you experiences but strips away your tendency to cling to them. They point you back again and again to the stillness beyond fire, bliss and illusion.

Why do some disciples develop sexual feelings towards the guru? How does the guru help them overcome this?

This is a delicate area. When Kundalini awakens, powerful feelings of bliss, love and intimacy arise. Many disciples confuse the guru's unconditional love with romantic or sexual attraction. This is not their fault; it is simply the mind's way of interpreting something it cannot understand. A true guru is not disturbed by this. They know it is part of the process.

True guru–disciple love is pure and unconditional. If it slips into projection and neediness, it becomes a trap. Some teachers avoid constant close contact with the disciple because the mind can twist devotion into attachment. With time and clarity, the energy purifies, and the disciple's love becomes pure devotion without confusion.

Kundalini and Self-Realization

In your case, did self-enquiry help complete the Kundalini process?

Yes. Absolutely. Without self-enquiry, I would still be lost in the endless play of energies. Kundalini alone can open visions and powers, but these still belong to the realm of the mind. It is self-enquiry, as pointed to by Ramana Maharshi and echoed by Gautamji, that brings the mind to its end.

Through enquiry, one directly sees that they are not the body, nor the mind, nor the emotions. After that, what remains is pure Awareness. When Kundalini rises to the crown and then descends into the Spiritual Heart, the journey is complete. This is where surrender is total, and grace carries one into realization.

Why do I fear losing the self?

This stage is the final barrier—the terror of annihilation. A seeker feels as though they are dissolving into nothingness, as if the 'I' that they had always known would not survive. And indeed, it does not survive with the death of the ego. What remains is vast peace, unshakable bliss and a freedom without limits.

Yet, before such an overwhelming dissolution, there often arise deeply unsettling and fearful experiences in meditation. These occur as the ego's rigid structure begins to collapse. Its foundations break down, preparing the way for its final disappearance.

Crossing this veil is like death, but it is the death of illusion. Life is then lived without fear, without the weight of 'me' and 'mine'. Existence is seen as a dream in the vast Awareness that is untouched by birth and death.

How is Kali related to Kundalini?

Kali is the fierce form of the Mother, the slayer of the ego. She wears skulls around Her neck—symbols of the words and concepts that bind us. In my darkest nights, I felt Her power stripping me of every illusion, every identity. It is terrifying, yet liberating. She destroys not to harm but to free. So, Kali is none other than Kundalini, or the Mother.

Is Kundalini awakening the same as Self-realization?

No. Kundalini awakening can prepare the ground for Self-realization, but the latter happens only when the movement returns to the Spiritual Heart and all seeking ends. Many believe that when the energy reaches the crown, enlightenment happens. But, in my view, it is not so. Unless you surrender to the Spiritual Heart, the play of phenomena continues.

Self-realization is when grace descends, when all concepts, experiences and even the desire for liberation dissolve into silence. Kundalini is a process; Self-realization is the end of that process.

Guidance, Teachers and Transmission

What is the likelihood of being misguided, intentionally or unintentionally, by healers or teachers? For instance, can Shaktipat given by someone who is not fully realized cause harm?

Not everyone who speaks of energy or healing is realized. Many are themselves caught in *maya*, mistaking their experiences for the Truth.

Only one who has gone beyond suffering and duality, and rests in Awareness, can truly guide others. A teacher still bound by the ego cannot lead anyone to freedom. If Shaktipat is initiated by someone who is imbalanced or not fully realized, the seeker may receive a surge of energy without proper guidance. This can disturb the subtle system and cause psychological, emotional or physical imbalance because the awakened energy is not being directed with wisdom.

What kind of disturbances can occur from such an imbalanced transmission?

The seeker may experience overwhelming fear, heat, restlessness, insomnia or even hallucinations. Instead of moving towards peace and clarity, they may feel trapped in heightened states of agitation or confusion.

Why does this happen?

A true master has stabilized Kundalini in themself. Their presence ensures that the transmission carries balance, grace and wisdom. But if the one giving Shaktipat has not completed their own journey, they unconsciously transmit their own imbalances to the seeker. This is why the seeker may feel disturbed rather than uplifted.

Many teachers offer 'weekend Kundalini activations' or short retreats promising awakening. Are these safe?

No, they are dangerous. Kundalini is not a technique or a weekend thrill. It is the Divine Mother's fire. Once awakened, it does not stop. The short-term course comes to an end; however, the Kundalini process continues, day and night, for years.

When the energy is stirred forcefully in a two-day workshop, seekers are often left unprepared. They return home with no grounding or guidance and no understanding of what is happening. Sleepless nights, emotional upheavals, fear and even psychosis-like states can follow. Without a true guru's ongoing support, many seekers collapse into confusion or despair.

I have met seekers who underwent such courses. They were promised bliss and light; instead, they found themselves unable to cope with surges of heat, fear or strange visions. With no teacher to guide them afterwards, they suffered alone. This is why weekend awakenings are reckless.

But don't these courses sometimes give blissful experiences?

Yes, initially. The energy, when artificially pushed, can intoxicate with bliss, lights and visions. But this sweetness does not last. After the workshop ends, the energy continues its work of dredging up fears, karma and buried emotions. If there is no proper foundation of surrender and guidance, the bliss quickly turns into fire.

The real path is not about chasing weekend highs. It is about walking steadily through both bliss and fire until the ego is dissolved. That requires patience, surrender and continuous guidance—not quick thrills.

Why do genuine teachers avoid promising quick results?

Such teachers know the reality, as they have walked through years of burning, visions, despair and surrender. They know that awakening is not a product meant for spiritual entertainment.

They emphasize readiness, purification and surrender but not instant experiences.

In my own journey, Gautamji always discouraged fascination with experiences. He pointed me back to stillness, the ordinariness of life and surrender. This steady pointing anchored me. Without that, I too might have been lost in chasing more highs.

You say weekend courses are dangerous. But are all practices wrong? Can techniques like kriyas or pranayamas help stabilize Kundalini?

No, all practices are not wrong. Certain kriyas and yogic techniques can help, but guidance from a realized guru—who has walked through the entire Kundalini journey and completed it—is of prime importance.

Why? Because a teacher who is not Kundalini-completed cannot see where you truly stand. They may push you into techniques that stir energy but do not balance it. But in the case of a true guru, the practices are prescribed with precision, according to your stage, temperament and capacity.

Ascending vs Descending Energy

What are ascending energy processes, and why are they not considered as safe as descending ones?

Ascending practices, such as certain pranayamas, bandhas or chakra-activating kriyas, are not always safe because Kundalini is often pushed upwards through effort, will or mental interference. Breath control, visualizations, bandhas or forceful yogic techniques may succeed in driving energy upwards, but this frequently happens without first stabilizing the nervous system and brain centres.

Although these methods may produce strong energetic movement, they can overstimulate the subtle system. The result may be excess heat, pressure in the head, emotional disturbance, loss of grounding, insomnia or mental instability. This occurs because the subtle channels and the left and right hemispheres of the brain may not yet be harmonized to receive and distribute the awakened force safely. When energy is pushed upwards prematurely, it bypasses the necessary preparation required for balance, often leading to discomfort rather than clarity.

What are descending energy processes, and why are they safer?

Descending practices, such as receptive kriyas, devotional breathwork or surrender-based meditations, allow energy to settle downwards from above. For instance, in the practice of the Eight Spiritual Breaths taught by Santosh Ma, energy first moves into the brain, where it influences the negative and positive polarities of the left and right hemispheres, dispelling dullness and passivity. Through this process, the entire nervous system is energetically restructured so that it can support the smooth and natural ascent of Kundalini.

In descending energy systems, the movement begins from the crown and flows into the brain, then into the heart, and subsequently, into the lower chakras. This downward settling balances the subtle channels and provides better integration. Rather than overstimulating the system, the descent cools, stabilizes and harmonizes it. As the upper chakras are gradually purified through this process, the current is able to rise later with ease and grace. Without this balance, energy may remain trapped in the lower centres, leading to agitation, strong sexual urges, emotional turbulence and confusion rather than genuine transformation.

Does it mean that one should never attempt ascending energy practices?

Without proper preparation and guidance, ascending practices can indeed be dangerous. Traditionally, they were introduced only under the close supervision of a realized teacher. In certain situations, gentle ascending practices may help clear a blocked *nadi* (energy channel) or release deeply held impressions, but they must be applied with great discernment and care. Like medicine, the same method can heal or harm depending on timing, dosage and the condition of the system.

Descending energy practices, such as the Integral Yoga of Sri Aurobindo, are considered safe because they are designed to purify the *Ida*, *Pingala* and Sushumna channels. This preparation ensures that when Kundalini rises, it is not overwhelming and does not meet resistance within the system. For most seekers, surrender remains the safest and most direct approach, allowing awareness to settle and stabilize first so that any upward movement occurs naturally, without strain or disturbance.

It is also important to understand that experiencing intense energy does not necessarily indicate spiritual evolution. Individuals with a very clean and well-prepared subtle system may experience little dramatic sensation because there are fewer blockages. In such cases, the process unfolds quietly and smoothly, reflecting balance and maturity rather than intensity.

Common Challenges in the Kundalini Process

Physical and Energetic Phenomena

During my Kundalini process, I feel intense burning, and sometimes, my whole body feels as if it's on fire. What is happening, and how do I deal with it?

The fire is one of the most common and most difficult phases of Kundalini awakening. When the current rises, it purifies the body and mind. Old karmic impressions, suppressed emotions and deep-seated fears are 'burnt'. This can manifest as heat in the spine, burning sensations in the body, headaches or even a feeling of being cooked alive from within.

I, too, went through this. Nights of sleeplessness, shaking of the body as if struck by lightning and excessive sweating in the absence of a fever. The mind thinks, *This is unbearable; I may go mad or even die.* But what Gautamji reminded me was very simple and life-saving: 'Do not fight the heat. Do not try to control it. Let it burn what it must. The Mother knows exactly what She is doing.'

When I stopped resisting and surrendered, something shifted. The heat was still there, but it no longer felt like punishment. It became a fire of purification.

But practically, can I do something to cool down when the heat is unbearable?

Yes, some simple things can help the body cope while the inner process continues:

- **Surrender mentally**: First and foremost, accept the heat as grace. Resistance makes it worse.
- **Stay hydrated**: Drink cool water, coconut water or herbal teas that calm the system.

- **Eat foods that ground you**: Eat simple, cooling foods (fruits, milk, rice, greens). Strict fasting or spicy foods can intensify the fire.
- **Rest in stillness**: Lie down or sit quietly, without trying to push the energy anywhere.
- **Maintain contact with the earth**: Sometimes walking barefoot on grass or sitting quietly under a tree can help ground the energy.
- **Take cold showers or apply cold compresses**: A very simple but effective way to calm the body.
- **Avoid manipulation**: Do not force pranayama, chakra visualizations or 'cooling' yogic techniques. These usually backfire. When my Kundalini first awakened through trataka, I threw myself into all sorts of ascending-energy practices that I could find in books—pranayamas, *beej mantras*, spinal breathing and bandhas. Instead of grounding me, they left me more unbalanced and unsteady, and at times, the energy grew so fierce and violent that I felt I was playing with fire. Mixing different pranayamas and mantras without proper guidance was not only confusing but also deeply destabilizing.

  It was only in 2021, when I met Gautamji, that a shift began. In his presence, I stopped trying to manipulate the energy and began to surrender. That was the first time I felt a sense of balance and safety after years of turmoil.

I cannot sleep properly since the time Kundalini awakened in me. Nights are filled with energy, tremors or visions. Is this normal?

Yes, it is common. When the current is strong, the nervous system is overstimulated. The energy moves like lightning, and the body cannot easily rest. I, too, went through long nights of insomnia and trembling in bed, sometimes not sleeping at all.

Gautamji's supportive words, 'Don't fight the night; even wakefulness is part of the process,' helped me endure these long, restless nights. The more I resisted, the worse it became. When I allowed the night to be what it was, a quiet acceptance entered. Here are some things you can do to counter insomnia:

- Keep the body cool by taking a shower and wear loose cotton clothes.
- Avoid stimulants, such as coffee and heavy food, late at night.
- Start doing gentle grounding practices, such as walking barefoot and focusing on the present moment.
- Don't turn sleep itself into a demand. Rest in awareness. Even without sleep, awareness is refreshing.

Over time, the current settles, and natural sleep patterns return.

My appetite has changed. Sometimes, I feel no hunger at all; at other times, strange cravings appear. Why?

Kundalini reorganizes the whole system, including digestion. The body may reject heavy foods, meat or excess spices. Cravings for cooling or grounding foods, such as fruits, tofu or cream, appear. For me, there were weeks when only fruit and milk felt possible, and sometimes, I felt the urge to consume more grains or salt.

The key is to listen to the body without fear or rigid rules. Let the energy decide. It knows what fuel is needed. If your appetite disappears, eat light but nourishing food, such as soups, fruits and grains, in small quantities. If cravings for certain foods arise, you can have them if they ground you; however, see that you don't overindulge in them. Remember, diet patterns do not follow your likes and dislikes now. They are meant to support the body while the energy is doing its work.

Do not panic; digestion usually resets naturally once the energy stabilizes.

I feel bodily pains (especially in the spine), head pressure or heat waves. Is my health in danger?

Many seekers panic when they undergo such physical 'ailments', thinking something is wrong. I too consulted doctors, but tests did not show any corresponding illness. These symptoms are often not medical but energetic. Kundalini works through the nervous system by opening channels. Pressure in the head, heat in the spine and sudden aches are common. This is what you can do to support the process:

- ❖ Address the symptoms through medical care if they are severe. But if the tests are clear, relax.
- ❖ Support the body by taking sufficient rest, stretching, exercising and walking in fresh air.
- ❖ Consume cooling foods and hydration as they help relieve heat.
- ❖ Most of all, surrender. The body is being reshaped. Trust the intelligence of the process.
- ❖ It is important to remain discerning and grounded. Kundalini can bring unusual experiences, but not all unusual experiences relate to Kundalini. True wisdom lies in knowing when to seek medical advice. Ignoring serious symptoms under the assumption that they must be spiritual in nature can be dangerous. Spiritual practice and medical care are not opposed to each other; both can serve you when used appropriately.

I sometimes feel like I am in an earthquake or that my body is expanding and shrinking. Why?

Kundalini alters body awareness. The nervous system recalibrates, leading to distortions—a sense of becoming tiny or gigantic, or of being 'here and, at the same time, not here' or a feeling as if the ground itself is shaking. These are temporary shifts in perception.

Ground yourself by looking at ordinary objects and naming them aloud, walking barefoot on grass, taking long walks, touching solid surfaces and breathing steadily until balance is restored.

I experienced a lightning-like jolt, like my whole body was electrified. Was that dangerous?

Many people report lightning surges, buzzing or sudden electrification. It can feel overwhelming, even ecstatic. These are powerful bursts of Kundalini clearing channels. Usually, they pass quickly. Support yourself after these episodes by resting, drinking water and staying quietly present. If such jolts recur too often, spend more time in grounding activities, such as walking, cooking and doing light chores.

I suddenly saw lights—flashes and even colours raining down. Are these real visions?

Many seekers see coloured lights, flames or even moving forms like snakes or symbols. They can last for weeks or months and are genuine phenomena arising as a result of Kundalini awakening, but they are not the goal.

To minimize these phenomena, rest the eyes often, avoid overstimulation and gently anchor yourself in the body (touch the feet to the floor, or take short walks). Visions will rise and fall; Awareness remains untouched.

My body jerks and shakes, and spontaneously performs yoga postures I never learnt. Should I stop this?

These are spontaneous kriyas. The energy moves the body into mudras or asanas to release tension and deep-rooted karmic impressions. If these movements are harmless, let them complete. If they are too forceful, lie on your side, place a hand over your belly and breathe slowly until you become calm. Avoid forcing or suppressing them; they are self-regulating.

Emotional, Psychological and Sexual Upheavals

I experience waves of fear and despair, and even feel like I am going crazy. How do I handle this?

This is perhaps the hardest part. Kundalini not only brings bliss; it also brings up buried fears from the subconscious. Nights of terror, sudden panic or even the sense of going mad are not unusual. When this happened to me, Gautamji would remind me, 'You are not the fear. You are the Awareness in which fear arises.' Slowly, I saw that even the darkest fear comes and goes. What I am, remains untouched. You can use these pointers to guide you on the journey:

- ❖ Do not fight fear. Let it pass like a storm.
- ❖ Anchor in the 'I Am', the sense of being, without stories attached to it.
- ❖ If despair comes, whisper inwardly, *This too is the Mother. This too is grace.*

Fear is the ego's last defence. When it dissolves, freedom dawns.

My relationships and social life feel impossible. I just want to withdraw from them. Is this part of the process?

Yes. As Kundalini works, the old personality feels out of sync with worldly roles. Friends and family may not understand and may worry about you. I, too, withdrew often, needing silence more than company.

This is natural. But complete isolation is not needed unless you are guided to do so by the guru. Stay simple: Reduce unnecessary socializing, but keep healthy connections wherever possible. Speak honestly with loved ones, explaining to them that you are going through a transformative process.

Remember that this withdrawal is not meant to reject life but to allow space for inner integration. In time, balance is restored.

Will these struggles ever end?

Yes. Every phase runs its time. The fire burns until it burns what must be burnt. Appetite, sleep and emotions find a new balance. What feels unbearable now will, at some point in the future, be remembered with gratitude because it was through this very fire that illusions were stripped away.

Grace is always present. Even in the struggle, the process is not against you. It is for you.

Since my Kundalini awakened, sexual energy has become overwhelming. Sometimes it feels uncontrollable. What is happening?

Kundalini stirs every layer of conditioning, including sexuality. The same life force that rises as bliss in meditation also moves as sexual energy. When channels are not yet purified, this energy can get directed towards fantasies or desires.

I, too, went through this. Sometimes, the energy rose as devotion, and, at other times, it manifested as raw sexual urge. The key to restoring balance was Gautamji's explanation: 'Energy itself is pure. It is the mind's interpretation that turns it into desire.'

Instead of suppressing or indulging in it, simply witness the movement. Let the current flow upwards by witnessing the movement of the energy. With time, the raw charge transforms into devotion, compassion and blissful stillness.

Sometimes, uncontrollable or even blasphemous thoughts arise against God, the guru or sacred figures. Why is this happening?

Kundalini dredges up everything hidden in the subconscious: not just desires but also anger, fear and rebellion. When the ego feels threatened, it can project ugly or blasphemous thoughts.

A seeker had restless nights when such thoughts stormed through his mind. He felt ashamed and afraid: *How can I think this about the very one I love?* But Gautamji reassured him, 'These thoughts are not you. They are clouds passing through. Awareness itself is untouched.'

The more you see them as the mind's play, the less power they have over you. Eventually, they fade, leaving only stillness.

How should I deal with guilt about these energies and thoughts?

One needs to see clearly that guilt is just another layer of the ego. The Mother is not shocked by your thoughts. She is the one raising them to the surface so that they can dissolve.

Instead of fighting or judging, whisper inwardly, *This too is You, Mother. I surrender to it.*

- ❖ Do not suppress the guilt, as it makes the energy heavier.
- ❖ Do not indulge in it as it strengthens the habit.
- ❖ Simply witness it, surrender to it and let it pass.

Over time, what once appeared as 'lust' or 'blasphemy' is transmuted into devotion and silence.

Does journaling help navigate the Kundalini process?

Journaling during the Kundalini (or deep meditation) process is profoundly helpful because it provides a safe and grounding outlet for the intense inner experiences that arise. As the energy awakens and begins to clear old patterns, emotions and memories from the subconscious, writing helps bring unconscious material into conscious awareness. By recording sensations, insights, dreams and emotional shifts, one can observe recurring patterns and gain clarity without getting lost in them.

Journaling transforms overwhelming inner currents into something tangible and manageable, allowing reflection rather than reaction. It also serves as a sacred dialogue with the Self—a space where intuition, fear, bliss and transformation can coexist and be understood in the light of awareness. Over time, these written reflections reveal the deeper trajectory of spiritual growth, helping the practitioner stay balanced and compassionate while trusting the process.

Understanding Different Experiences and Practices

What is the difference between a Kundalini awakening and a pranic surge?

A Kundalini awakening is a profound and irreversible opening of the dormant spiritual energy at the base of the spine. Once awakened, Kundalini does not switch on and off; it remains active 24/7, silently reshaping body, mind and consciousness. This process unfolds in waves and stages, often bringing deep purification, ego dissolution and a movement towards Self-realization.

A pranic surge, on the other hand, is a temporary rush of prana through the nadis. One may experience heat, tingling, vibrations or blissful currents, but it is not the full awakening of Kundalini. Such surges may come and go depending on one's practice, breathwork, meditation or emotional intensity, and they usually subside without long-term transformation.

What is meant by 'spiritual shopping'?

'Spiritual shopping' is a term used to refer to seekers who try or experiment with practices from different teachers and traditions, mixing them without proper guidance. It often comes from restlessness or the desire for faster results.

Why is mixing practices dangerous?

Each practice is designed within the context of a particular path and is meant to be done under the guidance of a teacher who understands its effects. When combined with techniques from other systems, it can create a lethal cocktail. Typical examples are mixing breathwork, mantras and energy practices. Instead of bringing about a balance in the practitioner, they confuse the subtle system and overstimulate the mind.

What kinds of imbalances can this cause?

The seeker may face insomnia, excessive heat in the body, anxiety, uncontrolled visions or erratic surges of energy. In severe cases, it can lead to psychological disturbance or a collapse of physical health.

What is the safe alternative?

Choose one authentic path and stay with it consistently. Under the guidance of a true teacher, practices can be undertaken in the right order and intensity. Depth, steadiness and surrender are what bring transformation, not the accumulation of methods.

Energy Stagnation in the Lower Chakras

Why does energy get stuck in the lower chakras?

The lower chakras carry unresolved karmic impressions, desires and fears. If these centres are not purified and the energy is forced upwards, the blockages resist it. The result is that the awakened force becomes trapped, creating agitation, imbalance or even long-term disturbance.

What complications can arise when energy is stuck in the lower chakras?

The seeker may experience uncontrollable sexual urges, fear, anger, depression, heat in the pelvic region or obsessive thoughts. Physically, it can manifest as digestive issues, reproductive problems or chronic fatigue. Psychologically, it can cause anxiety, mood swings or even psychosis in extreme cases.

For those who have not had a Kundalini awakening but find their energy repeatedly stuck in the lower centres, often expressing itself as strong sexual urges, compulsive thoughts, or restlessness, the key is to neither indulge in it compulsively nor suppress it forcefully. Instead, the energy can be allowed to transmute naturally through right channels. Simply witness the sexual energy as energy, without labelling it as good or bad. Also, regular physical exercise and a *sattvic* diet play an important role in such cases.

Are those teachers who are not Kundalini-completed the cause of this problem of stagnation?

Yes. When such teachers have not fully traversed and integrated their own awakening, they lack the experiential wisdom needed to guide others safely. They may teach powerful ascending techniques without understanding how to balance, ground and descend the energy, leading seekers into unnecessary turmoil. Furthermore, many public gurus are often personally inaccessible to sincere seekers and are thus unable to adequately address the complex questions and energetic challenges that arise along the path.

How can this be avoided?

The key is to never rush or force the upward movement of energy. When guided by a realized teacher, Kundalini rises naturally and safely, cleansing each chakra as it ascends. True guidance emphasizes surrender, balance and integration, and not reckless stimulation.

Ego Death

Why does the death of the ego—when the mind falls silent and all inner noise dissolves—feel so terrifying, as if we are losing ourselves, although it is a step towards awakening?

When the mind grows quiet, the ego begins to panic. It has spent a lifetime defining itself through thought, identity and stories. Silence feels like death to the one who survives on noise. Yet, the reality is that what truly dies is not you, the true Self, but the imagined self—the 'I'— that believed itself to be in control.

The ego's disintegration is mistaken for loss because we have identified the 'I' with our roles, stories and memories. When these begin to dissolve, there's a sense of groundlessness akin to free-falling into the unknown. But the unknown is not empty; it is full of the same life that breathes us.

In the Silence following the ego's annihilation, the vastness of Being reveals itself, not as something gained but as that which is ever-existing. The mind trembles because it cannot hold the Infinite, but once we surrender, we recognize Being as home.

As Gautamji says, the person fades so that Presence can rise to the foreground, and it is love that receives you on the other side of fear. What feels like dying is, in truth, the first breath of freedom.

Guru Parampara

Why is it important for the guru to be connected to an authentic Guru Parampara (lineage)?

A self-taught teacher may speak well and sound convincing, but when Kundalini brings violent energy surges, fear, ego inflation or prolonged dark night phases, only someone who has walked the entire terrain themselves and has been guided by their guru can recognize—without panic, projection or misinterpretation—what is happening with the disciple. Such guidance does not come from ideas but from lived clarity.

In a lineage, guidance does not function only at the psychological or physical level; the presence of the masters of the parampara continues to operate at the astral and causal levels, especially when the seeker's mind is unstable or overwhelmed. In a traditional lineage, the understanding of Kundalini is refined over generations, and its masters stabilize themselves in it. In turn, the guru helps the disciple stabilize their Kundalini experience not by controlling it but by removing interference in the entire process.

In my journey, Kundalini did not stabilize through techniques or control. It settled through trusting the guru and resting in his presence. Performing *sashtang namaskar* at my altar, meditating on the guru's form or watching his videos grounded me. They were not practices but ways of abiding in and surrendering to the guru's instruction.

There were moments when visions of Nisargadatta Maharaj, Santoshji and Gautamji arose spontaneously and provided a constant sense of being held and taken care of. They created a safe field in which Kundalini could do its work without destabilizing the mind or body.

With love and gratitude, I bow to Your divine feet.

Unity of Kundalini and Advaita

The journey of Kundalini is often spoken of as fire, upheaval and transformation. And indeed, for me, it was all of that. It shook me to my core, stripped away my sense of self, dragged me through nights of despair and enticed me with visions and powers. Sometimes, I thought I would not survive it. At other times, I believed I was chosen for something extraordinary. Both extremes were traps.

What saved me was the light of Advaita, coming into my life through the presence of Gautam Sachdeva. Kundalini exposed my shadows; Advaita dissolved them in the light of Awareness. Kundalini broke down every illusion; Advaita revealed that the Self was never bound in the first place. One was fire, the other silence. Together, they became a complete path.

My story could have ended in collapse, delusion or despair without Gautamji's teaching: 'Do not chase experiences. What comes and goes is not real. You are not the doer. Be still, be nobody.' These words anchored me when powers intoxicated me, visions terrified me and insomnia left me trembling. They reminded me that the goal is not the experience but freedom from identification with all experience.

In this unity of Kundalini and Advaita lies the hidden grace: Kundalini purifies, Advaita liberates. The fire strips away the false, the Silence reveals the Eternal. For seekers walking through this storm, the highest teachings of Advaita can serve as a lifeline, just as they did for me. They do not make the fire less fierce, but they reveal that beneath the fire lies a ground untouched—the Self—radiant, unbroken, free.

To all those who are having the Kundalini experience, I say, 'Trust the process while not losing sight of the Self. Do not cling to bliss, fear or visions. Allow the fire to burn, and let Advaita remind you of the Awareness in which it all unfolds. The true culmination is not a life free of fire but a life lived in the unshakable peace of what you already are.

It [Kundalini] is the same as *vritti* of the form of God (Bhagavatakara vritti) of the *bhaktas* and vritti of the form of Brahman (Brahmakara vritti) of the *jnanis*. It must be preliminary to Realization.

—Ramana Maharshi
***Talks with Sri Ramana Maharshi,* Talk 392**

An Appeal to the Medical Community: Accept and Understand Kundalini Awakening

Many people all over the world are (understandably) frightened and confused as a result of the experience of Kundalini awakening. They visit their general health practitioners and hospitals, or confide in their therapists, to find a solution. Such people often describe waves of heat moving through their body, flashes of inner light, powerful sounds that seem to arise from within, sudden movements they cannot control or the sense that their very self is disintegrating. To those medical personnel who are unfamiliar with the Kundalini terrain, these experiences resemble symptoms of psychosis. And so they classify them under medical terms, such as schizophrenia, bipolar disorder or schizoaffective disorder.

Once such a label is given, a cycle begins. Strong medications are prescribed, and sometimes, even electroconvulsive therapy is resorted to. It is assumed that such 'patients' will undergo their 'illness' for a lifetime. Unfortunately, this fatalistic approach compounds their pre-existing despair. The drugs may dull their awareness, but they do not touch the essence of what is happening.

Little do these practitioners know that what they diagnose as a psychological disorder is often the raw force of Kundalini at work. Although this misdiagnosis is unintentional and they have the patient's well-being in mind, the fact remains that it doesn't ultimately help the patient.

Transformation or Trauma?

The workings of Kundalini are not something new. Kundalini awakening is a process described in spiritual traditions for centuries. It is the rising of life energy that purifies, transforms and, ultimately, dissolves the rigid structures of the ego. It can bring both joy and terror, as well as visions of light and nights of darkness. To someone not in the know, this looks like an illness.

However, to one who has walked through the process, it is clearly the beginning of awakening. The tragedy is that modern medicine rarely considers this possibility. By reducing such experiences to a pathological state, the chance of undergoing a spiritual transformation can turn into unnecessary trauma.

The Role of the Medical Community

This is not an appeal for doctors to reject medical understanding but, rather, to expand its scope. When 'patients' report experiences resembling Kundalini awakening—waves of heat, vivid inner imagery, shifts between bliss and despair, or spontaneous bodily movements—it is, of course, essential first to consider the possibility of underlying neurological or psychiatric conditions. Yet, once these possibilities are ruled out by means of established diagnostic procedures, it is important to remain open to another dimension of understanding.

Medication may sometimes ease the intensity, but it cannot bring the process to completion. What truly helps is guidance from those who have already walked through Kundalini themselves and come out the other side in stillness and Self-realization. Such beings are empathetic to the sufferers' dilemma and know how to support them rather than suppress their symptoms.

Kundalini awakening is not an illness to be cured. It is a doorway to be honoured. It asks for patience, understanding and wise guidance. If our medical community develops the humility to open up to the possibility that there is such a thing called Kundalini, that it is real, and that realized guides hold the key to navigating it, then it can become a true ally in human transformation. Physicians could ensure safety, while realized beings could offer the road map for the inner journey. This simple partnership could prevent years of unnecessary suffering and give hope to those suffering from despair.

Glossary

Words appearing in italics can be cross-referenced within the glossary.

A

Advaita	A Sanskrit word that translates as 'not two' or 'no second.' This gives the idea that the inner *Self*, or Atman, is the same as the Absolute Reality, or Brahman; non-duality
amrita	The 'nectar of immortality', sometimes tasted during *Kundalini* awakening
Amrita Nadi	A subtle channel through which *amrita* flows during the descent of *Kundalini* from the crown to the Spiritual Heart, stabilizing realization as *Sahaja Nirvikalpa Samadhi*
asana	A steady *yoga* posture that prepares the body and mind for inner stillness and supports the safe flow of *Kundalini* energy
Aum	The primordial inner sound heard during deep states of awakening. In the *Kundalini* process, it can arise spontaneously as a continuous vibration or hum, reflecting the underlying pulse of Creation itself

B

bandha	'Lock', in Sanskrit. The purpose of a bandha is to 'lock' the energy flow in and to a specific part of the body temporarily
beej mantra	A short, potent seed syllable—such as *Aum*, Hrim, Kreem, Shreem—that carries concentrated vibrational power. In the *Kundalini* process, a beej *mantra* can activate or intensify specific aspects of energy. However, its effects are strong and should be approached with awareness and guidance
bhajan	A devotional song with a spiritual or religious theme
bhakta	Devotee
bhakti/Bhakti	Devotional worship directed to one supreme deity; a religious movement, path or tradition emphasizing the mutual intense emotional attachment and love of a devotee towards a personal god and of the god towards the devotee
Bhastrika	A forceful *yogic* breathing technique ('Bellows Breath') involving rapid inhalations and exhalations. It generates heat and increases *pranic* movement in the body. During a *Kundalini* process, Bhastrika can strongly stimulate the energy and is generally not advised unless guided by a knowledgeable teacher

C

causal body	The deepest subtle layer of individuality where impressions, *karmic* seeds and latent tendencies are stored. It is the silent root of the ego-sense. The causal body is what gets purified as unconscious patterns rise and dissolve. Realization occurs when even this subtle layer becomes transparent, revealing the pure *Self* beyond all bodies
chakra	A wheel or disc; in *yogic* literature, one of the several centres of consciousness located in the etheric body, usually depicted as a lotus flower. They are high-powered vortices of energy, which receive the cosmic energy and act as transformers to regulate the force of that energy so that it may be used by the various organs of the physical body
chakra meditation	A practice that involves focusing attention, breath or *visualization* on the body's energy centres (*chakras*) to activate, balance or cleanse them. In a *Kundalini* process, *chakra meditation* can intensify energetic movements and should be approached with care as the energy itself will naturally work through the *chakras* without deliberate manipulation
Consciousness	Referred to as 'Brahman' in Hinduism, which is the Ultimate Reality or supreme cosmic power, often described as the unchanging, infinite, immanent and transcendent Reality that is the divine ground of all matter, energy, time, space, being and everything beyond this universe. It is considered the source and essence of the universe; *Self*

D

darshan	Beholding a holy person or a deity, thereby receiving their blessings; presenting oneself for viewing by devotees
Divine Mother	*Kundalini*; *Ma Kali*; *Shakti*
doership	The illusion that it is the 'I' who acts. This false ego-self is the root of bondage and suffering

G

gurdwara	A Sikh place of worship, literally meaning 'the *guru's* door.' It is a space for prayer, singing of *kirtan* (hymns) and community service
guru	Imparter of knowledge; one who dispels the darkness of ignorance; a spiritual guide
Guru Parampara	Lineage of *gurus* following a particular spiritual tradition

H

hasta mudra	A hand *mudra*, primarily used in Indian classical dance and *yoga*, to express meaning and guide energy flow
Hatha Yoga	A traditional system of *yoga* that uses physical postures, breathing techniques and energy practices to purify and strengthen the body and mind. Its aim is to make the body a steady, stable vessel for higher states of awareness
Heart Chakra	The Anahata *Chakra*, located in the centre of the chest, which governs our heart, lungs and limbs

I

Ida — One (the left) of the two main channels within the body through which *Kundalini* ascends, regarded as the lunar channel

J

Jeeva Samadhi — A state in which an enlightened being consciously leaves the body while still alive, entering deep absorption in the *Self*. Their physical body is often interred in a sacred spot, which becomes a powerful place of silence and spiritual presence

-ji — An honorific suffix attached to names to indicate respect

jnani — a sage; one who has realized the Self

Jyotirlinga — A Jyotirlinga is a devotional representation of the Hindu god *Shiva*. The word is a Sanskrit compound of 'jyotis (radiance)' and 'linga (sign).' The Siva Mahapuranam (*Shiva* Purana) mentions sixty-four original Jyotirlinga shrines in India, twelve of which are most sacred. They are called the Maha Jyotirlinga (The Great Jyotirlingas)

K

Kapalabhati — A rapid, forceful breathing technique ('Skull-Shining Breath') involving sharp exhalations and passive inhalations. It generates heat, energizes the system and clears mental dullness. In the context of *Kundalini*, Kapalabhati can strongly stimulate *prana* and may aggravate the energy if done without guidance

Karma/karma	The path of action; actions or the consequences thereof; destiny
karmic	Pertaining to *karma*
Khechari Mudra	An advanced *yogic* practice in which the tongue is extended back and upwards towards the nasal cavity. It is said to redirect internal energies and stimulate subtle centres in the brain
kriya	A spontaneous, energetic movement—physical, emotional or subtle—triggered by the awakening of *Kundalini*, or a deliberate one as part of *Hatha Yoga* or Kriya Yoga. Kriyas can take the form of an *asana*, *pranayama*, *mudra* or a subtle vibration that purifies the subtle system and *chakras*, along with the body, breath and mind
kundal	Coiled up
Kundalini	The primordial cosmic energy, also known as the Serpent Power. It is the fundamental life force and, at the same time, the supreme spiritual energy usually lying dormant and coiled three-and-a-half times at the base of the subtle spine. The word 'Kundalini' is derived from the Sanskrit word '*kundal*'
Kundalini Yoga	The branch of *yoga* which is inner-directed and is concerned primarily with the awakening of *Kundalini* and the consequent spiritual experiences

M

Ma Kali	A fierce and compassionate form of the *Divine Mother*, symbolizing the power that destroys ego, ignorance and inner darkness. She represents transformation through fire—the cutting away of what is false so that the Truth can shine
Mandukya Upanishad	One of the shortest yet most profound Upanishads, which exclusively explains the nature of *Consciousness* through the symbol '*Aum*'. It explains the four states of awareness: waking, dreaming, deep sleep and *Turiya*
mantra	A word or sound repeated to aid concentration in meditation. 'Man' means 'mind' and 'tra' means 'to liberate'. A word or sound having a mystical power
mantra japa	'Japa' means the repetitive chanting of words or sounds (*mantras*) which liberate us from the mind
maya	Lack of knowledge of the *Self*; appearance or illusion
mudra	A sacred and symbolic gesture found in *yoga*, Buddhism, Hinduism, and Jainism. The most well-known mudras are used during *yoga* and meditation practice as a means of channelling the flow of vital life force energy known as *prana*. The term translates from Sanskrit as 'gesture,' 'mark,' or 'seal'

Mula Bandha	A *yogic* 'root lock' created by gently contracting the muscles at the base of the pelvis. Traditionally used to direct and stabilize *prana*, it can intensify the upward movement of energy

N

nada	Inner sound perceived in deep states of meditation
nadi	An etheric channel for energy flow within the body. Out of a total of 72,000 nadis in the human body, there are 100 major ones. Among these, there are three main nadis: Pingala, or the solar nadi, on the right side of the spinal column; Ida, or the lunar nadi, located on the left side; and the most important one of all, the central nadi, *Sushumna*, the vehicle of the balanced energy flow indicative of spiritual growth
Nirvikalpa Samadhi	Absorption beyond thought and form, but temporary; refer to *samadhi*

P

Pingala	One (the right) of the two main channels within the body through which *Kundalini* ascends, regarded as the solar channel
prana	In *yoga*, Indian medicine, and Indian martial arts, 'prana' is the Sanskrit word for 'breath', 'life force', or 'vital principle'. It permeates reality on all levels, including inanimate objects. In Hindu literature, prana is sometimes described as originating from the Sun and connecting the elements

pranayama	The *yogic* practice of focusing on the breath. In *yoga*, breath is associated with *prana*; thus, pranayama is a means of elevating the life force
pranic	Pertaining to *prana*
Pranic Healing	A no-touch method of healing yourself and others by using powerful and simple energy techniques given by the school's founder, Grand Master Choa Kok Sui

Q

Qigong	A traditional Chinese energy practice that combines gentle movements, breath and awareness to cultivate and balance qi (the life-force)

R

Ramana Maharshi	A great South Indian sage (1879–1950) known to a global community of spiritual seekers
Reiki	It comes from the Japanese words 'rei', meaning 'universal', and 'ki', meaning 'life energy'. It is a type of energy healing
Rudra Granthi	The intricate psychic knot at the Ajna *Chakra*, or the Third Eye *Chakra*, located in between and just above the eyebrows

S

Sahaja Nirvikalpa Samadhi	The natural, effortless state of abidance as pure Awareness while functioning in daily life

Sahasrara Chakra	The Crown *Chakra*, located at the top of the head, which connects us to the Universal *Consciousness*
samadhi	A union of the individual soul with the Infinite Spirit—a state of oneness and complete absorption
samskara	A mental impression, recollection, or psychological imprint of past actions. It is a 'deep groove' formed in the mind by repeated actions. In Hindu philosophy, samskaras form the basis for the *karma* theory
sashtanga namaskara	A type of namaskar (gesture showing respect) where you lie flat on your stomach with all the 'angas', or body parts, touching the ground
satsang	A Sanskrit term derived from two roots: 'sat' meaning 'true' and 'sangha' meaning 'community,' 'company', or 'association.' It can be translated as 'associating with good people' or simply 'being in the company of Truth'
sattvic	Pertaining to sattva, which is a Sanskrit word meaning 'light', 'goodness' and 'purity'. The quality of sattva is said to be life-giving to the body, mind and spirit
Self	*Consciousness*
Shakti	'Energy' or 'power', often used to refer to Goddess Parvati, Lord *Shiva's* consort, and considered to be His alter ego. In Hinduism, She is the primordial Goddess or *Divine Mother*, who possesses all riches, all strength, all fame, all beauty, all knowledge, and all renunciation, and is the Creatrix of the universe

Shakti Peetha	According to Hindu mythology, Lord Vishnu cut Sati's lifeless body into fifty-one pieces using the Sudharshan *Chakra*. The pieces fell at fifty-one places on Earth, which turned into fifty-one *Shakti* Peethas. Each *Shakti* Peetha is dedicated to a particular form of Adishakti, or the First Supreme Energy
Shaktipat	Transmission of energy or grace from a *guru* to a disciple by means of a touch, a look or *mantra* initiation
Shiva	One of the holy triumvirate of Hindu mythology, the Destroyer, the other two being Brahma, the Creator; and Vishnu, the Preserver. Other commonly used names of Lord Shiva are Mahadeva, Shankar, Jagadeeshwar and Mahesh; according to Shaivism, Shiva is *Consciousness* Itself, the absolute reality, and the source of all creation. Shiva is not just a god, but the fundamental 'is-ness' from which all existence arises and to which it returns
siddha	It means 'one who is accomplished'. It refers to perfected masters who have achieved a high degree of perfection of the intellect as well as liberation or enlightenment; an individual who, through sadhana (spiritual practice), attains *siddhis*
siddhi	Psychic and spiritual ability and power

spinal breathing	A guided *yogic* technique that involves moving attention and breath up and down the spine to circulate *prana*. While intended to balance energy, it can strongly stimulate *Kundalini* and intensify symptoms if done without proper guidance
subtle body	The mental, emotional, and spiritual body; the body not visible to the eyes
Sushumna Nadi	The central *nadi* through which *Kundalini* ascends and descends

T

Tai Chi	A slow, flowing Chinese martial art that harmonizes movement, breath and awareness to cultivate balanced life-energy
tapas	The practice of penance to grow spiritually and, ultimately, attain *Self*-realization
Tarot	A set of illustrated cards (typically 78 of them in the classic Tarot) used for divination, meditation and spiritual guidance
trataka	A classical *yogic* practice of steady, unwavering gazing used to purify the mind, awaken inner perception and strengthen the *subtle body*. Although commonly taught as jyoti trataka (candle-gazing), trataka includes any technique that focuses the eyes and, therefore, one's attention on any single point, internal or external, until the mind becomes one-pointed and thought subsides
Turiya	Literally, 'the fourth'. It refers to the 'fourth' state beyond waking, dreaming and deep sleep

U

Universal Mind	The collective field of thoughts, symbols, memories and subtle phenomena that exists beyond that of any single individual. It is the vast reservoir from which visions, synchronicities, psychic impressions and intuitive insights arise

V

vasana	A subconscious inclination formed from our *samskaras*, taking the form of likes, dislikes, physical and mental urges, desires and feelings. Unlike *samskaras* which we cannot identify or single out, vasanas are identifiable
Vedanta	An influential school of Hindu philosophy primarily based on the Upanishads, a set of ancient scriptures that are part of the Vedas. Vedanta, which literally means 'end of the Vedas,' explores concepts like *Self*-realization, Truth, and Ultimate Reality, and encompasses several sub-schools, each interpreting the scriptures differently
visualization	A mental practice of creating images or scenes in the mind to direct attention or energy. In the context of *Kundalini*, visualization can strongly influence *pranic* movement and may stimulate the *chakras* or inner experiences. Because it is an active, mind-driven technique, visualization can intensify the process if used during an awakening. It is generally discouraged unless guided, as the energy itself knows what to clear and reveal without mental interference

vritti	modification of the mind

Y

yoga	An ancient physical, mental and spiritual practice originating in India. It involves a series of postures, breathing exercises and meditative practices aimed at promoting holistic health and bringing about union (yoga) with the Supreme Being, or liberation
yogi	A practitioner of *yoga*
yogic	Pertaining to *yoga*

The author may be contacted on email:
kunwarkiranjit@yahoo.in

For further details, contact:
Yogi Impressions LLP
1711, Centre 1, World Trade Centre,
Cuffe Parade, Mumbai 400 005, India.

Fill in the Mailing List form on our website
and receive, via email, information on books,
authors, events and more.
Visit: www.yogiimpressions.com

Telephone: (022) 40115981, 22155036
E-mail: yogi@yogiimpressions.com

Join us on Facebook:
www.facebook.com/yogiimpressions

Join us on Instagram:
www.instagram.com/yogi_impressions